This edition first published on 13th March 2019

The author asserts her right to be identified as the editor of this work under the Copyright, Designs and Patents Act 1988.

ISBN: 9780244461539

ACKNOWLEDGEMENTS

I could not have done any of this without the help and encouragement of a small group of friends. The five school friends who kept me laughing even though they sometimes despaired of my latest disaster. Libby, Char, Fer, Susie and Jilly, thank you for your support. Thank you to my son James for our Sunday phone calls and his unfailing support and advice, and to my daughter Kate, because I have driven her nuts far too often.

Last of all, but never least, to my friend Paul who has worked so hard on my behalf and who was brave enough to publish the rude bits, a great big thank you for everything. I could not have done it without you.

FOREWORD

Where do stories come from? In my own case I had a thriving business at the Quaker boarding school I attended selling what can only be described as a precursor to Fifty Shades of Grey, although my knowledge of male anatomy was a little hazy at the age of twelve. An early departure from said boarding school led to a stint at art college and then on my long suffering father's insistence to Miss Marie's Plumtree's Academy for Young Ladies in Leeds. Attempts to earn an honest crust met with varying degrees of success until I thankfully married at the tender age of twenty. I spent the next 20 years happily hunting on Exmoor and flirting with the local farmers. I returned to art college, my husband having died and a degree of common sense having kicked in, as I now had two young children to think about.

It was my second husband who gave me the confidence to actually get a meaningful job at the ripe old age of 49 when the infamous Rose West trial began and I was taken on by SKY and HTV as a court artist and later as a police artist, those being the days before technology took over from talent.

I spent the next 12 years travelling the country and working harder than ever before in my life, covering trials and coaxing descriptions out of frightened victims, both of which I was surprisingly good at. I also took commissions for portraits. At long last I had found my niche.

After my second husband died I began a series of diaries written for five old school friends in the sleepless small hours and it was these five ladies who encouraged me to keep writing after I moved to Cornwall four years ago.

Where do stories come from? Most of mine are based on the truth with a bit of tweaking should honesty become a problem. The characters I use are on the whole a likeable bunch and drawn entirely from my imagination, so I apologise if you think you have met any of them. You haven't. Any similarities to persons, living or dead, is purely a coincidence and certainly not intentional.

CONTENTS

BABY..OR THE FISHERMAN'S DAUGHTER

Baby was known by two names. Firstly, of course, Baby, because that was what she was and secondly, The Brat, which was what her daddy called her. Baby soon learned that Daddy was the enemy. He did not want to play 'peek a boo' or watch baby cartoons with her, and if she dropped one in her nappy he fled the room, retching dramatically, which drove Mummy nuts. At an early age she learned to play one off against the other and so even at only eight months old, she was a dab hand at manipulation.

However, this particular sunny summer's day it came about that Mummy suggested to Daddy that he took Baby fishing with him. Baby could play on the bank in the sunshine whilst Daddy dangled his bait over the river. Mummy wanted a bit of peace and quiet and after all Baby belonged to Daddy just as much as to Mummy and it was bloody-well time they bonded. Little did Mummy realise exactly what bait Daddy would be dangling.

So it was that a disgruntled Baby was strapped in her car seat along with her favourite toy, Pink Bunny. She didn't like the look of this: Mummy not getting in the car with them and, worse still, she was packing food and milk and nappies whilst a scowling Daddy loaded his fishing gear into the boot. This looked sinister. The Brat twinkled at Daddy in an attempt at flirtation but he took no notice.

She tried one of her toothless gurgles which normally had everyone cooing over her, but this time it simply made Daddy want to reach for the sick bucket. Rage set in.

"Right," thought The Brat, "just you wait."

They drove through the Devon lanes in silence until they reached Daddy's favourite fishing place. It was a sheltered spot with hay bales piled up against the hedge and a soft bank on which Baby could play nicely. She tried her hardest to arch her back and make it well-nigh it impossible for Daddy to lever her solid little body out of the car seat, but she was no match for his strength and he soon had her slung over one shoulder in a very undignified position. He then dumped her on the rug.

"Shut up," he muttered.

Baby responded by glaring at him through narrowed blue eyes.

Just as she was attempting to regain some composure before deciding upon her next move, a girl came around the corner from where they had left the car. Baby's ears pricked up. Who should it be but Silvie, the pretty girl who looked after Baby when Mummy and Daddy wanted a night out.

"Great," thought Baby, beaming winsomely at Silvie whilst trying to signal frantically the need to be cuddled and rescued and patted. What a relief! Of course, Mummy would not abandon her to the ministrations of someone cruel enough to refer to her as 'The Brat'.

Silvie, however, was not best pleased to see Baby. Her face fell and she turned to Daddy in horror.

"What the f...?"

Daddy looked mortified and gabbled something about quality time and Mummy going out and, look, we could tie her to a tree perhaps? Baby most certainly did not like that thought and opened her mouth to bawl. Why was Silvie not her friend anymore? Why was she here? Sitting on the rug, with Pink Bunny clutched to her chest, Baby sobbed. Loudly.

"Oh for goodness sake," muttered Silvie as Daddy tried to kiss her. "We can't do anything with her sitting there. Thank God she can't speak yet. Let's feed her and see if she settles. Time is precious and waits for no man."

Silvie finished her homespun philosophy and, softening towards Daddy, wrapped her arms around his waist.

Baby watched. What was this all about? She was the one Silvie cuddled and read stories to, not Daddy. Why did Daddy need a cuddle? Would Daddy be put on the naughty step and then perhaps Baby and Silvie could play together like always. How could Baby get Daddy onto the naughty step?

Food was unpacked and distributed and Baby made sure she ate all the worst things she possibly could. She had a plan, and managed to consume all the grown up stuff like pickles, rich pate, miniature trifles from Waitrose, chocolate with fruit in it and egg sandwiches. Daddy had really pushed the boat out. Best of all she managed to filch most of Daddy's beer, which was disgusting, but needs must and emergency measures were necessary. All this was achieved without Daddy or Silvie noticing as they were too busy locking their mouths together. They were rolling around on the rug and Baby wanted the squeaking to stop. And why were Daddy's hands going up Silvie's little skirt? Surely she didn't need a change of nappy, did she?

"Oh, oh," cried Silvie, "I love you. Let's run away together. We belong to each other, and your wife can look after The Brat and we only need to see her every other weekend!"

Daddy hesitated. This was not quite what he had in mind. A roll in the hay was one thing, but it shouldn't carry with it the need to gallop off into the sunset. And Mummy had her good points. Or she did before The Brat came along. In fact, everything was The Brat's fault. Mummy was often too tired for sex and even when she wasn't too tired, there was always a wail from The Brat's room and Mummy would have to rush off, leaving him all fired up with nowhere to go.

He looked up and met Baby's eyes. He felt a stirring of something warm. Was it guilt? Baby gazed at him, thinking poor sod, talk about stupid, she had the upper hand now. Silvie was making noises about tying Baby to a bush with some binder twine they had in the car. No way was Baby going to stand for that, and even Daddy didn't appear too keen. He was looking at The Brat as though he had never seen her before.

"Did he need help too?" she wondered.

Wriggling her frilly pants and the nappy underneath so that there was a large gap down the side, Baby raised her plump little bottom as far as she could. Drawing in as deep a breath as her little lungs would manage she let all the air go down through her body until it reached the point of no return. Oh, what a wonderful feeling! The mass of chocolate, bananas, trifle, sandwiches and beer gathered force and shot out of her body like a cannon, splattering Silvie and Daddy with a spray of liquid manure. What joy! How satisfying! To make things even more disgusting, Baby lay back on the rug, enjoying the warm, slushy feeling that what had not exited further down was now creeping up her back, so that she felt as though she was lying in a warm bath. Perfect.

Silvie jumped up and screamed, "You little...." Whilst Daddy was actually rolling around and laughing uncontrollably.

"Don't you call my daughter a little..." he gasped between gales of laughter.

Silvie burst into tears as she tried in vain to scrub at her pretty skirt, her legs and her hair. Nowhere had escaped. The thought of having The Brat every other weekend was just too much and how dare he laugh at her? Bloody kids were all the same. Gathering up her belongings, she looked down at Daddy, who was still lying on the rug covered in sludge, laughing.

"I cannot see what there is to laugh at," Silvie exclaimed, trying to muster as much dignity as she could. "If you think I'm going to run away with you and have that Brat even for every other weekend, you must be joking. You don't love me. I'll never forgive you for this."

She stomped away, leaving a faint whiff of something horrible.

Daddy looked at Baby, who returned his stare. He saw her for the first time, almost apart from the ten minutes of euphoria when she was first born, and began to like what he saw. She was a baby but she was wise and she and he could become friends.

Baby stared back at him, trying her hardest to understand. But she also sensed that perhaps this was the beginning of a long friendship.

"Job done," she thought, and Pink Bunny nodded his head in agreement.

MY FRIEND AMBER

I sense something is going on. I was up, woken from my slumbers last night and watched over my friend Amber, who was stretched out on the kitchen floor breathing the deepest of breaths. We are friends and have been for many a year, ever since I first arrived and she took me under her wing and made me feel at home. We have done a lot of things together, Amber and I. We kept a vigil for three long nights and three long days when our much loved master was leaving us. He left us far too soon. He hadn't done nearly all of the things on his to do list, but we don't have much choice in the matter, something we understand much better than our humans, who seem to try and live forever.

Our home was picked up and we were taken to somewhere else to live, which was a long way away. I liked it, but Amber was homesick until she made some friends. I don't need friends.

But something was afoot. I saw my mistress kneel on the floor and whisper to Amber, who lifted her poor tired head a little bit and wagged her tail before sinking back down again. I sat and waited. Some other humans came and sat in the conservatory and then Ewan turned up and they sat some more, talking softly. Amber lay in the garage where it was cool and she was happiest. And I waited.

Eventually, nice Mr. Vet arrived with a lady carrying stuff. I don't know what it was.

Amber staggered to her feet and wagged her tail and they said "are you sure?" My mistress nodded and when nice Mr. Vet watched how Amber had to be helped up the steps, he said, "Yes, you're right. It is time."

They all came into the conservatory. The sun was shining and it was time for my morning sleep, but I had to stay. Ewan and my mistress knelt and took Amber in their arms and held her close. And then she was gone. Just like that. She was gone. I watched and waited and then I padded over to where she lay and I breathed all around her head and her face, and her beautiful brown eyes, which were slowly closing. I said goodbye to Amber.

And now I am top cat. I rule. I sleep on the bed, I have caught two mice which I presented to my mistress and I jump on her head every morning at five o'clock demanding breakfast. Life is good. I am a cat and I am wise enough to know that life goes on.

THE AMYLOID GANG

We were known as The Amyloid Gang in the hotel. Eight of us: four patients and four 'carers'. Also in the hotel were various refugees from the hospital across the road, trailing drips and dialysis machines and with arms covered in bits of sticky plaster where blood had been taken. And then there were the bona fide tourists and heaven only knows what sort of surreal situation they thought they had landed in. A bit off really, when you've booked a city break and there are people wandering around who are patiently dying in a dignified kind of way. I hope the tourists got a refund.

The main topic of conversation amongst The Amyloid Gang was whether you had to pay for your trip to the Royal Free, and as the answer was usually 'no', we marveled at the generosity of the NHS. It had provided a free car all the way from Wiltshire and was now putting us up in a reasonably good hotel, but I suppose it was because The Amyloid Gang were pretty rare and therefore worth spending a bob or two on to further any research they had in mind.

We arrived and it was straight in there with a nice chap pushing David in his wheelchair which I seemed to have no control over whatsoever when it came to my turn. Arriving on the third floor at the tiny Amyloid department we were filled with anticipation.

This was going to be the answer to all our questions. No more pussy-footing about;

14

this was going to tell us everything we needed to know. They knew the answers, they were the Royal Free, the experts in this field. There were endless tests that first afternoon and David was weary after his journey, but that was what he was there for and what he had to go through to get the answers that we needed to have.

Blood pressure was taken, sitting and standing. He was meant to stand for three minutes to see how his blood pressure went, but he couldn't. The nurse panicked as he sank nearer to the floor despite putting all his weight on my shoulders. And I whispered Amber's name to him, told him he had to take her for a walk, had to stay upright, had to find the strength somehow. But he couldn't. And he sank to the floor as the nurse rushed off in panic. Next came the famous scan. The highlight of everything, the scanner was going to tell us what we needed to know. Sitting in the corner room were two young medics behind glass doors so they weren't zapped. No such treatment for yours truly, just a chair in one corner for me to perch on. David started to slide into the scanner and, lo and behold, what should come out loud and clear on the speakers but Ave Maria, which made me laugh into my handkerchief. All I could think of was that it was bloody tactless, but what a relief it was to laugh.

I looked forward to that evening as a respite and got a little scrubbed up in readiness. I hoped for a nice restaurant and a

15

glass of wine at the bar. David couldn't eat although he was hungry, because, unbeknown to us, his throat was closing up. It was being destroyed along with the rest of his organs by the monstrous amyloid alligator. He sat there as we tried ice cream and all sorts of things to no avail. And he was so tired. We went back to our ground floor bedroom and I wasn't strong enough to help him from his wheelchair and into bed, so the lovely receptionist came to help. No Health and Safety crap; she just came and helped.

The next day was the same. More tests, more not eating. I went for a walk through smart Hampstead and looked at people and bought a baby present for a friend because it was good to have a focus whilst we waited to be told what we needed to know. But I knew already. I knew in my heart but I was very calm and practical. When we went back to the hospital to hear what we needed to know, they told us nothing. Nothing except vague talk of forty-two weeks of chemotherapy, which was a total nonsense. He couldn't have done four weeks, let alone forty.

Looking back, they must have known that he was going to die, but maybe just didn't want to tell us what we needed to know. We were driven back to Wiltshire by a delightful man who, as we approached our village, became more and more freaked out because there were no street lights. This made us laugh and that was comforting.

And then the world went haywire. They never did tell us what we needed to know. They never told us anything. And then he was gone.

THE LOST SHEEP

Robert was a good little who absolutely hated his grandmother. She frightened him to death. She far preferred his older brother and, worst of all, every Sunday when the family joined her for lunch, they had to chomp their way through piles of nearly raw beef, which was dripping blood and had hardly seen the inside of an oven.

Granny Appleyard was an old Yorkshire woman, long since widowed and living in an atmosphere of mutual loathing with her bachelor son Eric, who was heavily into air hostesses and Mrs. Clarke, the long-suffering housekeeper who bore the brunt of her mistress's vindictiveness.

Granny paid an annual visit to Scarborough to see her other son, Bernard, father of Robert. Bernard could only stand so much of trips to the Floral Hall and the Tree Top Walk, and would then announce that he was working every evening and would thus be unavailable for the second week. This left poor Jeanne, his wife, in a state of suppressed fury, controlled only by the thought of the substantial inheritance coming their way.

Robert was in the school summer play. He only a small part, but for a little boy of seven who never got chosen for anything at all, it was a thrill. Robert was a sheep. It was unclear as to what a sheep had to do with A Midsummer Night's Dream but Robert was happy and learned his words, or bleats to more

18

accurate, along with the rest of the children. And the costume! It was a splendid affair, fashioned out of a sheepskin rug and a pair of antlers picked up in a junk shop. These were quite large and had to be practically nailed to Robert's head before they stayed put.

At long last the day of the school play dawned. Unfortunately, Robert's mother went into a decline after a particularly testing morning attempting to cut Granny's toenails. Granny was also in a tetchy frame of mind and announced that she would like to go shopping and Robert was to accompany her.

"But it's my school play this afternoon," wailed poor Robert. "We've had the day off to prepare and I shall be missed dreadfully!"

"Rubbish," retorted Granny, "you are only third sheep and they can perfectly well manage without you. They only put you in so as not to upset you."

The cruelty of the remark shook Robert to the core. Silently he tried to control his wobbling chin as he and Granny walked down to the bus stop, whilst his mother, feeling slightly guilty, slipped a fifty pence piece under his pillow. She did love him dearly but the temptation of an hour or so without the old bag was just too tempting. In silence they climbed onto the bus and in silence they sat there.

Granny was pleased with herself at the success of her plan to wreck Robert's day, but it was too much for the poor boy. Quick as flash he leapt to his feet just as the bus was moving off and ran for home, leaving Granny to sail away with no idea of her address, no mobile phone or anything else of use.

Some hours later the drama teacher was counting the cast. The audience was settling into their seats when there came a muttering from behind the curtain.

"Where is the third sheep? Has anyone seen the third sheep? We've decided to make him the lead sheep as Damian has stage fright. Where are you third sheep?"

There was a scuffling and in staggered sheep number three, his woolly coat sliding off his narrow shoulders, antlers at half cock, but oh, what triumph was written all over little Robert's face! He had arrived all on his own, two bus rides away, he had somehow managed to more or less climb into his costume and, best of all, he had outwitted Granny. His theatre debut was a triumph, especially when his friends heard of his escape. He was a hero.

Granny fared rather less well as, being unable to tell the police where she was staying, she had thrown a hissy fit and clouted a policeman, which resulted in five hours in a cell to cool off.

Robert's parents were secretly highly amused and both of them slipped him a fiver, with strict instructions to keep it a secret.

Granny Appleyard developed a grudging respect for her grandson and eventually left him all her money.

BISCUIT'S LITTLE SECRET

Her name was Marie, but she was known as biscuit. After her husband Derek had been inconsiderate enough to drop dead with a heart attack whilst playing golf, Biscuit's rather bossy daughter Elizabeth decided in her wisdom that it would suit her and her rather ghastly family if they built a Granny annex, using Biscuit's money of course. This would make it easy to keep an eye on her and make sure she didn't go on too many expensive holidays and spend all the inheritance or, worse still, remarry. They knew Biscuit was a pretty little woman who could tempt any old roofer if she put her mind to it. (A roofer is a gentleman of a certain age who targets lonely women, preferably widows, in the freezer department of Waitrose, hoping to be offered a roof over his head. Do keep up).

And so it came about that eventually poor little Biscuit was installed in her granny annex, away from all her friends and at the mercy of her daughter. Her son was miles away in London and rather kept out of things owing to his sister being prone to emotional meltdowns at regular intervals.

Biscuit was lonely. Any ideas she had of playing happy families with her daughter, whom she loved very much but was slightly wary of, were soon knocked into oblivion. Biscuit, never having lived near relations, was quite looking forward to being a perfect granny, dishing out pearls of wisdom to her adoring grandchildren and perhaps playing Scrabble or something similar. The actuality was that the grandchildren were usually plugged into something and had not the slightest interest in their grandmother's life history. What no i-pads, no texting, no mobiles? Totally gross and beyond comprehension! Whatever did they do all day? Play building dens? Oh how pathetic, thought the grandchildren and they kept out of the way unless they were short on the pocket money front, in which case they paid a perfunctory visit to see what Biscuit would come up with.

Her daughter worked long hours and her son-in-law, Brian, was a law unto himself in that nobody seemed to know quite what he did as there was little evidence of him doing anything much at all. But it was none of Biscuit's business and they seemed happy enough in their own way except every week they would tell her how busy they were and she could manage to put out the re-cycling, couldn't she? And go to Tesco's for them as they were SO busy? And could the four of come to supper tonight as it would save Elizabeth cooking after the fencing/swimming/extra maths/etc?

She began to realise that she would have to make her own life if she was going to survive. She recognized that, since the demise of the good Derek, her status had taken a bashing and she felt she had lost her position in the family food chain, and, most worryingly of all, she had lost her voice. Her opinion was either never sought or was met with that patronizing rolling of the eyes which our offspring tend to use when their aged and senile parents say something stupid. She felt she was treated with benign tolerance rather than the love and respect of earlier times. A feeling which comes to us all in the end did we but know it.

She began to take the local paper and discovered tea dancing. This was something she had long wanted to do but Derek could not be lured away from his golf, his bridge, his cookery lessons or, indeed, anything at all. One day, Biscuit dressed herself with great care, putting on one of her pretty floaty skirts which suited her so well, and a delicate little cashmere sweater. She crept down the road to the bus stop without telling anyone where she was going. She arrived at the Princess Pavilion in good time to enroll for a tea dance every Tuesday afternoon, colliding as she turned with a tall, good looking gentleman who caught her just before she tripped and promptly fell in love with her.

That was the beginning of Biscuit's secret life. She too fell in love with the tall good looking gentleman whose name was Peter. He was widowed as well, but there any similarity ended.   Peter had a beautiful old Victorian house overlooking the beach in Falmouth, and he drove an old Alvis with great panache. Peter had a boat and he was rich. Best of all, Peter was in love with his Biscuit. All summer long they danced every Tuesday afternoon from two till four and then they would take themselves off for a cup of tea. Over the next months they learned everything about each other, and this made them fall in love even more. They started stealing out in the evenings, which was more difficult as Peter would have to hide his beautiful car around the corner and hope it wouldn't get keyed, and Biscuit had to pretend she was doing a sociology course and take lots of paperwork with her every week, which was a bit boring.

She thought she was getting away with it, but the twelve-year-old grandson noticed she was looking suspiciously happy and pretty. He followed her one evening and saw her getting into the car with Peter. Shock horror! The inheritance! He went hot footed to find Elizabeth and tell her the alarming news. Part of him wanted to blackmail Biscuit because he would like some new trainers, but the thought of the lost inheritance haunted him, so he poured out this disaster to his mother who was, quite gratifyingly, horrified. She proceeded to blow the biggest gasket in living memory.

"Right," whispered Elizabeth through gritted teeth, "after all we have done for her!"

The fact that Biscuit did all the ironing, cleaned all the silver and shared the utility bills (divided unfairly by two instead of four, which meant she paid far more than she should have done) escaped her.

"Right," she repeated, fuming. The old peoples' home beckoned and the children could have the annex, which had been in her mind all along. She had already sourced an inexpensive home in the centre of St. Austell. It had quite a pleasant view if you ignored the council tip.

Oblivious to all this, Biscuit carried on with her secret life until, one day, greed got the better of him and the deeply unpleasant twelve-year-old decided he might as well cash in while he could. He popped in to see his grandmother to tell her that she had been seen with Peter.

"I could do with some more trainers," he whined to Biscuit, who knew what was coming. "It can be our little secret, Granny, and I won't tell Mum. A hundred pounds should do it. Cash."

Poor Biscuit cries. She was devastated. She knew she was being used by the family. She knew that the only good granny was a dead granny and she was heartbroken. The next afternoon she caught the bus as usual to the Princess Pavilion and fell into Peter's arms with tears pouring down her face.

"What can I do?" she sobbed, wiping her nose surreptitiously on his beautiful jacket. "I thought they would love me and look after me, but all they want is my money! The next thing they'd do is put me in some home for gaga old people and my life will be over."

Peter was no fool. He thought for a while and made some telephone calls because, though sort of retired, he had fingers in lots of pies. Unbeknown to Biscuit, he was well able to take care of himself and of her.

"Right," said Peter, after an hour or two. They had skipped dancing this week. "I have an idea. I love you. I would like nothing better than to live with you. Are you prepared to give up the annex to a tenant and is it in your name? You obviously can't sell it separately from your daughter's house, but there's no reason whatsoever that you cannot sub-let it to a tenant, all legal and above board and take a healthy rent from the council. I know a chap in the Housing Department, so let's do the legal stuff this afternoon and then I shall carry you away. Your wretched family are not the only people who can have secrets."

And so it was that a couple of days later, when everybody was out and all the legalities had been sorted, Peter collected Biscuit and all her belongings, included her cat. Then a rather grateful family, with ten children, three dogs and seven chickens, arrived with their belongings in plastic bags. They proceeded to set up an outdoors cooking contraption because they liked cook their meals in the fresh air.

Armed with a lifetime tenancy agreement, this deserving family settled into the annex and eight years later they are still there. They have had three more children and are very happy indeed.

Peter and Biscuit spend their time going on ballroom dancing cruises and entertaining their many friends. Sometimes in the middle of the night they sip their cocoa and giggle about the mess they left for Elizabeth and her truly awful family. They too have a secret. It is the secret of a long and happy life. The secret of love.

RAIN SONG

Many years ago, when I was a lot braver than I am now, I became the proud owner of a race horse whom I shall call Rain Song. Bred in what is known in racing circles as 'in the purple'; that is possessing an impeccable pedigree of amazing aunts and uncles winning all sorts of smart races. The only problem, and it was quite a large one at that, was that Rain Song had inherited none of the winning genes and trailed in last in every race she was entered for. As my father, who owned her along with three friends, said 'it wasn't that she couldn't go fast, it was simply that all the others went faster.

And so she offloaded to me because I lived in Devon and had a paddock and a couple of horses. The excitement when the horse lorry arrived soon turned to dismay when a skinny, weary little horse tottered down the ramp. A chronic skin infection had taken the shine off her coat and it was obvious that she had been kept at vast expense in an annex out of sight, which was a common practice for no-hopers kept at livery miles from their owners.

When my farmer neighbour clapped eyes on her he roared with laughter at this hat rack roosting in my paddock. However, when he calmed down and stopped chortling we began to work on her and kept at it all through the long summer days. Good in traffic, good to load, gradually she regained her confidence and her coat began to shine once again. She made friends with my horses and put on weight. People stopped insulting her and by September and the start of the season she was a credit to all our hard work and good feeding. She was ready to roll.

How lucky I was to have even been given a horse such as this little mare. How I could boast about her breeding, how smart I felt! And how great is the fall which comes after pride!

Having downed a swift whisky and hooked up with all my old hunting friends, her first hunt started promisingly enough. She trotted after all the other horses looking happy and confident and very pleased with life. The trouble began when we entered the first big field with all of us behind the Master, the penalty being death/expulsion/slow torture if one was ill mannered enough to overtake his lordship. Even Bedlington Farmers' hunt, a rag tag collection if ever there was, had its own standards. There were strict rules which one obeyed without question. Unfortunately, Rain Song knew nothing about the rules and the moment her dainty little hooves touched the grass she was off. She careered in a sort of crab-like sideways gait away from the field of riders and, ears pricked, nostrils flaring, snorting with excitement (her, not me) we charged across the line of the hounds, the Master and all of the horrified riders and landed up in the river, soaking everyone who got in her way.

As the day progressed there were regular shouts of 'look out, here she comes,' as we cannoned through the hounds, the huntsmen and the gleeful riders who very cruelly laughed their heads off when she lost her footing and deposited me in the river. After that little mishap Rain Song decided that water was not to her liking and I spent the next few hours trying not to sail over her head as she steadfastly refused to cross even the smallest puddle. Jumping over ditches and bushes was another hazard. Being a flat racer she developed a sort of double buck designed to unseat me before attempting an ungainly scramble over whatever was in the way.

But enough was enough. I had a reputation to live up to and when she banged her nose on a beam in the stable and became known as The Unicorn, I decided to call it a day. There is only so much humiliation a woman can take. I had taken her out with the hounds four times and each time she became worse. She had an absolute ball hurtling all over the countryside, but simply had no idea what was asked of her. It was hard to blame her as all her life she had been in trouble for not running fast enough and now she was expected to stay at the back. It was all too much for her little mind. She had to go.

Following a difficult conversation with my father and the other three owners, who failed to see why she could not just live in my field and have a nice time, she was off to Exeter horse sales. I did not enjoy doing that to her, but I don't believe in idle plant and she was too well-known for all the wrong reasons to be sold locally. She sold for five hundred pounds to a pony-tailed old Etonian from Crewkerne named Antony Trollop Carew, who sounded eminently suitable for a failed racehorse with an egg on her forehead and an impeccable pedigree.

I forgot all about her. And that was the last conversation I ever had with my father because he dropped dead two hours later in the home of his long-standing mistress after a day's hunting. What better way to die? It caused quite a stir, but that is another story altogether.

Several years later I went with spouse number two to watch some polo at Taunton. Like Bedlington Farmers' Hunt, it was rather splendidly scruffy with overweight red-faced farmers hammering around the field whilst trying to stay on their equally overweight ponies and hit the ball at the same time with varying degrees of success. Unusually, the ponies were named in the programme. Polo ponies are called ponies rather than horses. I do not know why, but there you are. You don't need to know much to fit in. Just sit there shouting 'well ridden orf' and everyone assumes you know what it's all about.

There she was. Rain Song. I could hardly believe my eyes and rushed off to find Mr. Trollope Whatnot, an avuncular gentleman whom I liked on sight. The egg on her head was gone. He told me that she was the best pony he had ever had and this would be her last season before she retired and had a foal or two. He said she was with him for life. I gave her a hug, which she shrugged off as if to show her disgust that I had failed her. It just took the right person to spot her potential and that person was not me.

Incidentally, it was Father's Day when I found her again. I like to think my father would have smiled and said 'I told you so.'

THOMAS, A LOVE STORY

Thomas lived under the bed. Thomas was meant to be a macho stud cat but somehow he simply could not get the hang of what he was meant to be doing, so he was sold and re-homed at half price by his exasperated breeder.

And he still didn't know what he was meant to be doing. He missed his two brothers. His new home was large and scary, so he continued to live under the bed. For three months he stayed there. Occasionally he would creep out and find his food bowls and spend a penny or two in his shiny new litter tray but, apart from these midnight sorties, he steadfastly refused to emerge from under the bed to sit by the fire or be stroked like any other cat.

Thomas was lost and his mistress was worried about him.

"Thomas is lonely," she said to her husband, "we must do something about it."

They went back to the cat breeder in Oxford and fought their way through the kittens rampaging around the house. They listened to the tales of woe about anti-freeze in the drinking water at cat competitions and they came home with a feisty little tortoiseshell queen whom they named Isabella. She was a confident little soul, and showed no fear whatsoever when released from her carrier. Thomas, true to form, remained under the bed until the husband went upstairs and shooed him out and brought him downstairs.

Isabella, rolling merrily around on the carpet, full of confidence and fun, took one look at Thomas and promptly came into season. Having never got this far Thomas was horrified at this appalling behaviour. He wanted to comfort her and stop this dreadful screeching, but he had lost his manhood and with it instincts. Head on one side, Thomas gazed at her and promptly fell in love. Hearts floated above his ginger head. Violins played, he crooned at his new love, he patted her with his little white paw, he circled her lovingly. The more he circled the more wanton she became. Thomas considered his options and decided to sit on her head, which pleased her not at all.

"Wrong end you idiot," she screamed in frustration. Still Thomas knew not what to do, but all night he sat with her, patting her and trying to groom her pretty coat, and all night she screamed. She screamed through the next day and the next until everyone, including Thomas, was shattered through lack of sleep. At the first opportunity Isabella paid a visit to nice Mr. Vet, so that life could return to normal.

Thomas loved her. Oh, how he loved her. He sat there beside her and watched her and she taught him lots of things. None of them stayed in his head very long, but at least he began to have a life of his own and no longer lived under the bed. Isabella would catch a bird and transfer it gently to Thomas's mouth,

34

whereupon he would open his jaws and the bird would fly away. Burmese are notoriously bad at catching anything, so the tally was pretty low but Thomas didn't mind. He was happy and that was all that mattered. Until the Day of the Carrier Bag.

The mistress, having been to the supermarket, had left all the orange carrier bags on the floor. Strolling contentedly around the kitchen Thomas took it upon himself to see what was inside said bags and squeezed himself into one. Interesting. All very fine until he decided to leave and found the handle was around his neck and he was thus attached to it. Panic ensued and suddenly there was an orange tornado hurtling around the kitchen, into the hall, into the sitting room and back into the kitchen where various humans were crying with laughter, which was a little unkind. The carrier bag did several laps of the circuit before hurtling up a large apple tree where it came to rest on one of the highest branches.

Thomas clung onto the branch, still attached to the carrier bag. What to do? No-one could reach him! Where was his soulmate? She was cowering behind the kitchen door utterly bewildered by the astonishing turn of events, but she had enough sense to realise she would have to do something. Creeping stealthily over to the apple tree she began to climb upwards towards the carrier bag. Was it going to attack her, she wondered? Thomas's head peered fearfully out of his prison and his face lit up when he saw Isabella making her way to him. Slowly she inched along his branch and managed to get the plastic handle between her tiny teeth. Thomas wailed in fear as she chewed through the piece which was around his neck. Suddenly, with one final jerk, she freed him. Now came the hardest bit. Going up had been borne of necessity but getting down was a completely different ball game. However, the humans who had been so unkind as to laugh at his adventure came to the rescue and, with Isabella's assistance, they managed to grab the scruff of his neck and heave him to safety.

So began the greatest love story between two cats which ever was. Isabella stopped flirting with all the other Toms when they visited the cattery. Thomas became masterful and pleased with himself. The only thing he never attempted to do was to climb trees. His four paws stayed firmly planted on the ground for the rest of his life.

OVER THE FENCE
OR
BASHER AND THE SUNSHINE GIRLS

It was such a tempting puddle just over the fence, especially as his mistress had forgotten to fill the home pond. Basher had been eyeing it up for some time but thinking and planning required energy and Basher was an idle chap. He was a very large Muscovy duck who lived in considerable comfort with his mistress Naomi and a gang of lower class Aylesbury ducks, who were kept for the table. Basher was a pet, not destined for the oven, but the same could not be said for his fellow Muscovies who, being male, had, one by one, disappeared, having been called to the invitingly warm interior of the cooker.

Basher studied the fence. He was too fat to squeeze between the rails and too heavy to launch himself into the air, even if he had known how. But oh, oh, what did he spy but a bale of hay leaning up against one of the gate posts! Without a moment's hesitation, he was up the bale and over the fence, squawking with excitement as he lumbered through the air.

But he landed in the road. And he didn't see the car until it was too late.

Naomi found him an hour or so later. A sorry sight, although it could have been worse. He had tried to crawl home dragging his poor, broken leg behind him but had unfortunately collapsed when he reached the safety of his garden. He looked up at Naomi who shook her head sadly.

"Oh, Basher, what are we going to do with you? You silly old thing. Let's see what we can do about that leg."

With her customary skill and patience, she located, in the chaos of the children's bedroom, a discarded lollipop stick which she strapped to Basher's leg as a serviceable splint.

Over the following weeks Basher learned to hop quite successfully and by the middle of the summer had no more need of the support as he could get around in a dot and carry manner. But he was lonely. He would not eat and just sat there turning his face away from the inferior ducks who were due for the table. He watched as they met their fate in the vegetable garden where the mistress swiftly slit their throats and left them to bleed onto the lettuces. She later realised she should have stunned them first, but that's another story. On hot days Naomi's father would arrive and sit with his daughter on the front steps for a plucking session. That was a tedious chore indeed, and Naomi always wore a bikini to stop the feathers going down her neck or into her knickers. But my mother would wail, tearfully, "I didn't bring up my daughter to behave like this." Naomi and her father took no notice.

Eventually, Naomi noticed that Basher was not thriving and realised he was lonely so, finally, after a lot of searching, she came home with no less than five adult lady Muscovies and let them out into the garden. Basher eyed them suspiciously until he realised they were for him.

Hobbling over to the nervous group, and before even having the courtesy of introducing himself, he mounted the nearest and had his wicked way with her. She was not too impressed with his lack of manners and, when she was released, she dusted herself off before stalking away in disgust. Naomi watched in dismay as one after the other of the newly found ladies received the same unchivalrous treatment. At last Basher was satisfied and had a little rest before consuming a large breakfast followed by a snooze in the sunshine. Over the weeks that followed the ladies learned, as countless ladies before them, to lie back and let the old boy have his fun while dreaming of shopping trips or rearranging the furniture in the duck house. And harmony took over.

Naomi christened them the Sunshine Girls because of the joy they brought to Basher, who led his little harem around with pride. He no longer had the urge to escape and because the old chap lived a very long time, many ducklings were produced. They were also allowed to claim squatters' rights on the green hall carpet when the weather became too warm, and never again did Naomi forget to fill the pond.

THE DIARY OF A HANDS ON GRANNY

Granny and Grandpa practiced what I suppose is known as Idle Grand-parenting. They liked (some of) their grandchildren well enough and, as always, the first one was a bit special. Generally, they could take it or leave it, so when they volunteered to have three of the six children for a week at half-term their friends were understandably highly amused.

The children actually enjoyed a bit of healthy neglect after the rigours of home and were much better behaved than when their parents were around as Granny and Grandpa ran the visit like a benign boot camp. The children regularly disappeared down to the stream where in one particular instance the heavens opened and they returned soaked to the skin but very cheerful. Granny and Grandpa had drawn the line at turning out to collect them They saw no problem in sodden children in February and, in any event, they were fast asleep in their armchairs by the time the youngsters returned. The children made some toast and put themselves to bed and everyone was very happy.

One day they all had to go to the hospital in Bristol as Grandpa needed to have some blood tests because he was about to be very ill, but no one knew that then. Granny had explained that poor Grandpa had to have a needle in his arm and the children were all in the back of the car, singing a rude version of

Postman Pat when the oldest one, who was around ten, muttered, "Grandpa isn't very child-friendly, is he Granny?" Granny had to admit that no, he wasn't, but she did point out that he liked children who were well behaved and had good manners.

"However," she went to say, "if you feel that Grandpa has behaved badly at any time, just think of him having that big needle stuck in his arm."

The conversation was forgotten for a day or three and off they all went in one big happy family group to the At Bristol Science Museum Day, for which Granny had spent a considerable sum of money as a treat. Unfortunately, the queues were so long that by the time they reached the entrance Grandpa was about to blow a gasket.

Wisely Granny parked him in the soft play area with the two younger children whilst she took the older one upstairs to look at various computers. That lasted all of ten minutes, the exhibits being so complicated that both Granny and her granddaughter were numb with boredom and non-comprehension and came downstairs. And what a scene met their horrified gaze.

Grandpa was standing in the middle of the sandy pretend desert clutching a plastic giraffe and trumpeting in frustration, whilst the two youngest children watched him with a kind of fascinated horror. How badly could he behave? Grandpas were not supposed to throw wobblies in public! Granny acted swiftly by going straight to the entrance office, where two ladies were eyeing the rumpus with detached amusement. They had, after all, seen it all before, but rarely involving adults which made it more fun. Granny reached them and, having recovered some of her equilibrium, said firmly that she wanted her money back.

"Oooh no," said one of the ladies, "all we can offer you is a free ticket to the aquarium next week, when half-term is over."

"Not on my life," retorted Granny, now on a mission to protect her family no matter how badly they were behaving. "He'll murder someone before long, and I cannot be held responsible for that."

The duty lady eyed Granny and realised she meant business. Reluctantly she handed over the fifty odd quid and smiled in a not unsympathetic manner as Granny mouthed her thanks before heading off to rescue her incandescent husband. By now he resembled a large hippo trying to get out of a very small pen.

"I know," she said, "let's go to that Italian place over the road and spend the money on a slap up lunch."

The suggestion was met with cries of glee from everyone and so they scampered across the road and piled onto the tall stools near the windows so they could see what was happening outside. The smallest child looked at her grandfather from under her fringe, which was almost covered with one of those dreadful knitted hats with plaits which dangle down. Coupled with green boots and an ancient camouflage jacket falling down past her knees, she was a picture of sartorial elegance.

Grandpa met her gaze and had the good grace to look slightly sheepish.

"Big needle for Grandpa," said the child almost too quietly to hear. But Granny heard and could not contain her laughter, which bubbled up from deep inside her. She laughed and laughed and almost choked over her glass of wine.

"Why is Granny giggling so much?" asked one of the children.

"Because Granny is rat-arsed," gasped their grandmother. She noticed the expression on her husband's face. "And what is more, she doesn't give a hoot."

JUST ONE MORE DANCE

The Parkinson Diaries.

Just one more dance, they kept saying, just one more dance, but I couldn't do one more dance however much I wanted to.

I met a man recently who wanted to dance with me. We went with friends to an amazing pub on the quay in Falmouth. Live music, great atmosphere, everything I love. And the man I was just beginning to know a little bit and just beginning to care about was with me. A very nice man. Interesting, but very private. The friends we were with whispered to me that they were seeing a different side to this man that night, they had thought he was cold but certainly that night he was anything but. He held me closely and we danced in a way that I have been dreaming of for three years and it was so good.

But gradually I could feel the concrete dripping into my bones. I could feel my spine turning to stone. I shoveled in as many more pills as I dared but to no avail. The man kept taking my hand and saying, "come on, come and dance." My friends kept saying 'go and dance' and nobody understood that my body was running on an empty tank, that the turning and whirling of the dancers was frightening me. Parkinson people cannot run. The sudden movements of whirling and turning and being spun around is terrifying to them.

And so I sent this good man to dance with other people and I watched with a smile on my face and envy in my heart.

Then it was time to leave and it took ages to get me out to the car. We went to a friend's house for coffee and I was nearly dead from exhaustion and smiling and being a good person. All the time, this man I was with kept hold of my hand and hauled me up and down the steps and was kindness itself, but that was not what I wanted and we drove home in silence.

When we finally got to my house he kissed me goodnight. I watched him go down the drive and I thought 'if he turns around I will see him again. He didn't.

Go away, nice man, I have nothing to offer you or any man. I may be alone but I have my pride. If he rings me today I will tell him that.

A PIECE OF PAPER

He sat down with a bump onto the chair which someone had produced. No mean feat on the side of a busy road. His head felt fuzzy and a bit hot and he wondered what was happening. He sort of remembered being yelled at by that grumpy man in the next bed. Something about peeing all over his bedclothes. There must have been a mistake, he would never do that. The man was plainly nuts. Why would he do that?

He felt gentle fingers extract the piece of paper from his top pyjama pocket and heard the relief in their voices as they read out his name and address. Yes, there was a wife; yes, he had gone on the run after an altercation with another patient. Yes, the ambulance was on its way and yes, he would be back in his hospital bed in two shakes of a lamb's whatnot.

He let himself drink the tea they brought. Where was his wife? He obviously had one, but he could only remember a girl with fair hair and a ready smile who had loved him a long time ago. He couldn't quite see her face but she must be somewhere nearby, so he thought that if he went back to the hospital she would come and find him and then he could go home. And finish that jigsaw puzzle he had started the other day. Yes, that's what he would do. It always paid to have a plan. That's what men did to protect their wives. They always had a plan.   Later.

The little old man was now in his hospital bed, his wife beside him holding his hand.

"Hello dear, what have you been up to?"

"Who are you?" asked the little old man.

"Why, my dear, I am Mary Jean. Your wife."

"No, you're not," he retorted firmly. He knew what was who and this was not Mary Jean.

"Oh, don't go having one of your turns, you'll only upset yourself," said Mary Jean. "Of course I'm Mary Jean. Who else would I be?

"You are not my wife," muttered the little old man.

"Yes I am. Now don't make me cross."

"My wife has fair hair and she smiles. Not like you. I don't know who you are. Go away. She's coming to take me home, away from here," protested the little old man. "She promised I could finish my jigsaw puzzle."

"I'm afraid not, dear," said Mary Jean. "You're in here for the long haul. I cannot have you escaping like this, and my name is Mary Jean. I shall go now, as you are making me very cross. I've come all this way because you ran away and got lost."

She leaned across to kiss him goodbye. He turned his face away. Who was this bossy woman anyway? Where was his lovely fair-haired wife?

The woman sighed and reluctantly prepared to leave the man she once loved and who given her so many happy years. As she slowly made her way out of the ward, a young hospital physio approached the little old man.

"Hello, Mr. Williams," he said. "I see your name is Samuel. Now then, do you prefer to be called Samuel or Sam or Mr. Williams?"

The little old man gazed at the newcomer.

"Who is Mr. Williams?" he asked.

THE LOOK OF BATH

Once upon a time to very best friends were strolling through the beautiful city of Bath following an extremely pleasant lunch in the Green Tree public house. Their respective chaps had adjourned to watch the rugby and ladies were thus free to wander at their leisure and admire the scenery.

One of the friends was a glamorous blonde of a certain age, but possessed of extreme self-esteem and not a little vanity. Her scarves were always tied just so, her scarlet lips always matched her scarlet nails and with her admirable body poured into her tight fitting jeans and high boots, she strode along exuding confidence. Whilst the cleverly tied scarf hid the fact that her embonpoint was ever so slightly crinkled, her artful application of the scarlet lipstick failed to recognise that sometimes less is more.

The other lady was just a friend. An easy going lady who had yet to realise that her very best friend would always disappoint her.

And it came about that a vigilant professional photographer who worked for a well-known fashion house spied the two ladies and immediately pounced. She blocked their path.

"Ah, the look of Bath. The very look I'm searching for. You have the look of Bath. Please let me take your photograph.

Immediately the glamorous one sprang into action. Out came her lipstick, which was never knowingly travelled without, not even when in later years she bailed out of an upstairs window in a fit of pique. She took up her pole position, leaning against the wall of the NatWest bank, whilst the friend, who was equally surprised and delighted, also stepped towards the bank and took up her own position with what she imagined to be a coolly professional smile. She thought how well she must have scrubbed up that day. Stroking their hair and straightening their linen trousers (this is, after all, the look of Bath) the two ladies preened and glowed with excitement.

Enter the photographer lady. Taking the friend by the elbow, she said loudly, "No, not you dear. Would you mind sitting on that bench over there while we photograph your friend?"

She gazed at the photographer thinking, 'well, she could have just pretended to take my picture, and maybe Melanie could have said it's either both of us or neither. But, hey, it makes a good put down story.' She duly sat down on the bench and watched while the photographer went about her professional business and tried not to feel just a little bit humiliated. Eventually, when the photographer had finished and cards had been exchanged and air kisses blown, the two very best friends linked their arms and continued to enjoy their afternoon stroll. And the friend laughed and told the story against herself, but it was the beginning of the realization that the

Glamorous One would always disappoint her.
Just like David said.

GUILTY AS CHARGED

There is so much to say. The words flow out of me. This is another story that seems to want to be written.

With every whispered 'guilty' in response to every count, the defendant's head drooped further down until his chin was touching his chest. Neat in his grey suit and white shirt, and the inevitable poppy because it's November and he hopes that the jury will be swayed just a little by his patriotism, that it might keep him out of jail. He knows he will suffer there as he has made other people suffer. Little people, small boys at a boarding school away from their parents, too afraid to tell. And the parents, thinking they were doing the 'right thing', the best for their sons; this is what middle class families do, they send their children away for a 'better education,' so they will be rounded individuals when they emerge. Not damaged, like these little boys who were so afraid. It wasn't even worth a new cricket bat, which is the standard bait to offer little boys who think they are invincible, but find out too late that they are not.

Sitting there as an observer, I could have been anyone. I watch his face, now hidden further into his shirt. I watch his wife, sitting next to the vicar, dragged along to improve her image, handkerchief clutched in hand and mouth quivering. How will she survive the embarrassment, the humiliation in the village? No smoke without fire, they will say. What about his own children? Did he have a go at them as well? How could she not have noticed? They will whisper and then when she goes into the village shop they will fall silent and look the other way.

I am just an observer, a non-person, a fly on the wall. I observe the faces, the reactions of the main players, so that I can record it in glorious colour for the news at six. I watch and as I watch I become aware that there is a young man sitting next to me. On one side I have him, on the other, access to the door for my hurried exit when it is over. I sense his anger, his desperate humiliation, his sorrow, his embarrassment that everything he suffered is being read aloud in cold clear words which cut into his soul. He is shaking. His hands in his lap shake and I lean over and take his hand and whisper in his ear.

"Hang on in there. I am with you."

And so he did. Clinging tighter and tighter to me through the next half hour as more and more charges were read out. The wife is in tears by now, and still the defendant's head hangs down even lower. He wants to be dead. He knows he is finished.

Finally, it comes to an end and the man is led below to start his sentence. It was a good trial, a fair result, people are pleased. I still hold his hand and his father leans across from his other side and says to me, "thank you for that, thank you so much." I nod and give the son a quick hug and then I'm gone to do my job for the six o'clock news. It's just a job. I see many trials and many victims, but he stays in my mind. I do something I have never done before. I walk out and away from the court. I do not want to see him later on the news and watch as he realizes I was not just an observer, that I was not there for him. I did not feel proud of my job then. He had enough memories. I did not want him to see a dumbed down drawing of someone who had hurt him so much. I didn't do the drawing. I went home instead and he has stayed in my thoughts ever since.

I hope he made a good life for himself later on. I really hope so.

ACCIDENT

The woman was driving along a country lane towards the M5 on her way to work as a Court Artist. She was a good driver and she sang as she drove towards Bristol, because it was the first day of a new trial and that was always nerve wracking and always exciting. She was a careful driver, but even the most careful of drivers could not have foreseen what would happen next. Suddenly seeming to fly through the air, ricochet off a tree and bounce back into the road was a small hatchback. She thought it was a dull kind of colour, sort of neutral but later she was told it had been blue.

Slamming on her brakes, she shuddered to a halt and quickly stepped out of her car and ran towards the hatchback. She had expected to see someone sitting there, shaken but unhurt and that she would be able to extricate him or her and continue on her way. The reality was different. A youth slumped over the steering wheel and was very unconscious. She seized the door handle and pulled. Nothing. By this time another driver, who had been behind her, had appeared. The woman continued to pull at the door to no avail. The man tried his best. Nothing. The car did not seem to be badly dented but perhaps the internal locks had jammed.

Then she saw something which frightened her. Flames were licking around the bottom of the windscreen inside the car. Small flames, but threatening. She thought of sparks flying to her own car, so she ran back and moved it back a few yards, as did the man who had joined her.

She reached the door and pulled again. The man tried again. Nothing. By this time the flames had caught hold and were meaningful. They licked all around the steering column and still the boy was motionless. The man backed off. The woman thought fleetingly of her own children, her husband, her home. Then she thought of the car exploding and taking her with it, but how could she leave him to burn to death? If, in fact, he was not dead already. The heat intensified and by this time a cameraman on his way to the same trial as the woman saw his opportunity and was filming the burning car. That's what you do if you're a freelance; you switch off from the emotional side and get on with your job, which the woman understood and did not judge.

She made her decision. She would be no use if she burned to death, or even if her hands were too burned to hold a pencil. She stepped back and the man who had tried to help put his arm around her as she trembled with fear and shock. And shame because she had put herself first and left him to burn.

The car exploded into a ball of fire, sparks and flames careering across the road, burning the tarmac and eating up the little car. The police came and did their bit. The woman and the other witnesses were gathered in someone's kitchen giving their statements. Then the woman got back into her car and drove down the M5 to Bristol and did her job. She trembled all day, but she did her job. At the end of the day she bought a bunch of daffodils to put on the spot where he had died, because she didn't know what else to do or how else to behave.

It was several days later that she cried and cried when her son telephoned. She cried because it could have been her son and because she had not been brave enough to save him. She cried because she was ashamed. She cried because she had put herself first.

THE WORST WEDDING THERE EVER WAS

It wasn't really my fault that after the weeks of autumn sunshine it rained. Or that the poor confused Baby of the Bride screamed blue murder throughout the service. Or that my daughter had offended the Groom by writing on the wedding cake 'HELP' in large red letters, or that most of the Groom's relatives had fallen by the wayside for various reasons, not least of which was a letter telling the Bride to 'bog off.'

No, I cannot be blamed for any of that. Had I known that the assembled guests were such a lackluster collection it would have saved me a great deal of money spent on a very beautiful purple velvet suit (which, in retrospect, made me look like a drag queen) and I would not have dreamed of a glorious decadent group of witty and good-looking guests wreaking havoc and dancing until dawn.

None of that was my fault, but I bore it bravely as usual.

What was possibly my responsibility was the wedding car. And what a wedding car! It started with a sense of relief that the father of the screaming baby was actually marrying my daughter. That had been a cause for concern. Call me old-fashioned but it is all too easy these days for a daughter to rock up, baby in tow, assuming that Granny would pick up the pieces. Not this Granny, who had only recent shed the shackles of motherhood herself. Not likely. My husband and I were prepared to overlook any shortcomings the Groom may have had and were thankful he knew where his duties lay.

The daughter, being a graduate of a somewhat leftish university, had pretty skewed ideas about global warming and 'wimmin's rights' and had requested a small wedding car to transport her from reception to pub that evening, for the less formal part of the affair. That wonderful moment when everyone kicks off their shoes along with their good behaviour and has a good time dancing and feeling sorry for those poor souls who only have an invitation to the evening jollies.

Coming home from Bristol one day with the wedding in mind (the daughter having handed over the entire matter to me due to work obligations) a thought crept into my mind. What if...after all, her invitations had been designed around one of the cartoons for which I was well known in a local kind of way.

"What if we did....."

"NO," said my husband. "Not a good idea," his mouth twitched as he poured me a glass of wine. A large one, due to the stress we were both under. "Well, maybe," he mused. "do we know her sense of humour, do you think?"

"Oh yes," I replied. "She hasn't got one."

That may sound unkind but even she admitted that herself. Maybe this was so far out that we would get away with it.

The idea was simple and certainly involved a small car. Nobody could deny that we had followed her instructions.

In the village lived an ancient grave digger who went by the name of Eerk. Well, it was meant to be Eric, but it never sounded like that. Eric had about four teeth, a urinary bag down one leg which he loved to show everyone, and a gloriously deadpan face. Most importantly of all, Eric had a Reliant Robin. And it was purple. Metallic shiny purple. I went down to the village to see him.

"Ere," he said, "ave you seen that bit of wallin' I done for they in the big 'ouse?

I had indeed. The whole village had turned out to inspect the way it wavered along the grass verge with stones sticking out in all directions. Eric was justifiably proud of his wall. But the owners were marginally less so when they were informed that they had employed the wrong Eric, his namesake being a proper builder down the road. Should've gone to Specsavers.

During the following weeks Eerk put in several requests for silver tinsel, silver balloons, silver bannisters and other stuff. I marched into town and asked for the worst white plastic roses they had ever seen, which the shop was delighted to offload. By the end, the car looked a treat. White silk pleated the back seat reminding us of Eerk's true calling as a gravedigger. The plastic roses, which Eric had kept religiously and lovingly watered until his moment in the sun, were most convincing and a tasteful arrangement had pride of place on the back shelf.

In fact, waiting for the arrival of the star of the show, I reflected that I was rather happy with my efforts and was just beginning to laugh when I realised that all was not well.

There was a kind of wailing noise coming from the hotel foyer and suddenly my daughter emerged, scarlet with rage and wailing like a banshee. Any thought that she might have seen the funny side were dashed as the wailing showed no sign of abating. Scooping up her long white dress in one hand and grabbing the baby with the other, she stomped up to the car and stood there waiting for the good Eerk to open the door for them both. Thankfully his urinary bag had held firm and he looked almost statesmanlike with his undertaker's top hat and black gloves. He helped the bride into the car and then looked enquiringly at the Groom who was doubled over with barely suppressed laughter.

"I'll never be able to come here again," hissed the bride to me.

"That's ok," I responded cheerfully, "you won't be able to afford it anyway."

This was hardly the most diplomatic of responses I admit but I was actually pretty fed up by this time. A great deal of effort and time had gone into the planning of this harmless jape and Eerk had been stalwart in his preparations. He deserved to be appreciated.

Back up the drive they lurched, Mrs. Eerk having appeared by this time to join the merry throng following the car. I learned later that some friends were waiting to throw confetti over the happy couple as they rocked into the village but, having caught a glimpse of my daughter's face, thought better of it and sloped off before they could be lynched.

And so ended the worst wedding ever. Apart from a few incidents in the pub when the bride's stepfather fell over and dislodged his toupee, we oldies danced the night away as only we oldies can, and Eerk and his purple Reliant Robin were never mentioned again. But they became legendary in those parts.

FROZEN

Same old, same old. Like that thing of where were you when Kennedy was shot, or Princess Diana was killed, or the Twin Towers, or, if you are pretty ancient and a bit of a saddo, the day Elvis died?

In this instance, the unforgettable incident was when one cold and frosty morning, a much loved pooch named Oliver sat down in his own driveway and his balls froze to the paving stones. I can hear you men shuddering with most of your adult lives being occupied with that part of your anatomy.

Oliver attempted to stand up, his stomach telling him it was almost breakfast time, but to his surprise and embarrassment he was stuck. He guessed that his nether regions were somehow attached to the ground and fear gripped him. He did what all dogs always do and emitted a long, forlorn howl of pure anguish.

Upon hearing the sound of a soul in torment his mistress rushed out to see what on earth could be wrong. She called to Oliver as he struggled valiantly to find his feet before collapsing onto the frozen ground. I'm sorry to say that she was heartless enough to laugh out loud. No sympathy there, then. Oliver looked sadly at her, and stifling her giggles, she looked back at him, her shoulder shaking with mirth. "Oh, Oliver," she sighed, "what are we going to do with you?"

Oliver gazed at her. His mistress thought for a moment. Boiling water was out of the question for obvious reasons, as was one of those blow torches that you use in the kitchen. She wondered about getting Oliver to lick his nether regions, but decided that his tongue would freeze as well and that would just exacerbate the situation. By this time several of the neighbours had gathered around to offer unwanted and tactless advice such as 'chop 'em off," amid guffaws and chuckles of amusement.

Oliver glared at the idiots. No more guarding their houses for free he decided crossly, forgetting that he had allowed at least two burglars into several houses over the past four years, so when he did get it right no one took any notice.

A small child squeezed in between the adult legs and stood looking down at Oliver, who was by now becoming increasingly hungry and cross.

"Ice cream," intoned the small child. "Smear it on his bits and it will form a barrier between them and his tongue. Then he can lick it off without fear of freezing. Simple."

Oliver's spirits rose. That sounded more like it, he thought. He was very fond of ice cream. But where to find it? A quick search proved unsuccessful. It being early in the morning, no one had any available.

Poor Oliver. His stomach by now was grumbling loudly. The mere mention of ice cream having set off a chain of noises worthy of a hungry lion, never mind a tubby middle-aged Labrador.

A hot water bottle! That was the answer! Pressed against his portly stomach, surely that would work? The small child was despatched to find one and came back a few minutes later clutching a pink bottle in her arms. Now for the difficult part, the placing of the hot water bottle underneath Oliver's tackle without causing him pain. Very gently his mistress, having now recovered her equilibrium, eased the bottle under the outer edge of his tummy. Oliver whimpered in trepidation which rapidly turned to relief as the hot water bottle started to work its magic. But not so fast! The ground was now so cold that the bottle soon ceased to be hot and started to freeze as well. Oliver was beginning to panic. His black nose dribbled, his eyes filled with tears of humiliation and fear. Was he here for the rest of his life?

But wait...was the sky growing a little bit lighter? Was that the sun creeping up over the yard arm? What is a yard arm? Slowly the warmth struggled into the frozen air, gradually the poor cold birds emerged from their sheltered corners of the garden, relieved at having survived another winter night. Slowly, Oliver began to thaw out too. Very slowly, because he was very, very cold and his skin was tender, the sensation began to creep through his body and after many minutes Oliver thawed out.

Breakfast he thought.

IN WHICH THEY CROSSED THE FLOOR

A sunny day in September. It was the step-daughter's wedding and the day was already fraught with danger even before everything kicked off. I was up in the hotel room and was thinking that I had got the 'step-mother as wedding guest ensemble' down to a fine art, when I caught sight of the daughter striding across the lawn below, wearing a pair of my jeans and a brown t-shirt. When she makes the effort my daughter can scrub up with the best of them, but one has to get the right moment and patently this was not it.

"Darling," I trilled from the upstairs window, "come and use my room to get changed in."

"I am changed!" came the reply.

Now, my husband's ex-wife is from a very smart family and her very smart Married to Hedge Fund chap and living in Geneva, was there with her adored sons who were, of course, suitably kitted out in blazers and chinos. You know the sort; they are the ones whose parents write those awful Round Robins at Christmas extolling the successes of their offspring. The sort of person one wishes just a little bit of bad luck to come their way. Nothing fatal, but enough to be life changing.

However, I knew that look on the daughter's face, so I backed off. Enough that she had turned up, her being in the throes of yet another rocky romance.

The son then ambled into view. I took one look at him and had to laugh. He was under a three-line whip to beg, steal or borrow a suit for the occasion and, sure enough, he had done as he had been bidden. And how. He was wearing a vomit green ensemble whose sleeves were halfway up his arms and the trouser legs of which barely covered his ankles. He loped past and gave me a cheery wave.

"Nice suit," I said.

There followed the nuptials, after which we all filed into a rather pretty dining room with a vaulted ceiling and took our places at the large square table with the smart seats all along the top. Now, here's the rub. On account of one or two issues, the two families had never been allowed to meet. Mistake number one. My step-daughter's new mother in law had just completed her second stint in Holloway for fraud so, as you can imagine, my husband, her father, was not exactly thrilled and caused further angst by refusing to make the speech welcoming the poor chap into the family. Mistake number two as it transpired that my beloved was seated between the bride, who was trying to rescue her day, and his ex-wife who terrified the life out of him.

To add to the jolly mood of this happy day, the ex-wife was in full Grieving Window mode, her latest lover having dropped dead outside the Fire Station. Not a good atmosphere.

Eventually the meal lurched to an end. The bride made a rather pointed speech whilst her father squirmed in his seat. He was later caught on video muttering "thank God that's over," which didn't help matters. Steve the Fence and the jailbird shared a glance and you could see that they were sick to death of the whole thing. They kept themselves to themselves, which was just as well as the relatives of the bride were studiously ignoring the poor things.

We filed through a double doorway into the disco room with its flashing lights and chairs all around the walls. Steve the Fence and the jailbird sat as still as could be, clutching their drinks and looking desperate. The ex-wife was busy sobbing into her hanky and people were standing around beginning to look bored. A ten year DJ began to turn the tables, but still no-one moved and you could have cut the chill in the air with a knife.

And then it happened. My son, in his puke green suit and Doc Martins, and my daughter in her brown t-shirt and her mother's jeans strode into the room. Without hesitating they made their way across the room to where Steve the Fence and the jailbird were sitting.

My offspring introduced themselves and asked them if they wanted to dance. They stood up and allowed themselves to be escorted onto the floor. The four of them danced and as they did so they smiled and others began to drift onto the floor. The day was saved.

I was never more proud of them than at that moment. Vomit green suits and brown t-shirts don't matter at all, it's what inside them that counts. It transpired over the years that the jailbird and the good Steve had a remarkably strong marriage, despite spending a couple of years apart every now and then. If you remembered to put the silver away when they came to visit, they were actually very good company.

THE GREEN GNOME OF CRYSTAL PALACE

We arrived horribly early for Christmas to discover our hosts at a crucial stage of culinary preparation, sweating and stressed in a hot kitchen. David excelled himself by spraying dog biscuits all over Sarina's beautiful turkey and destroying the lock on the bathroom door. We had the distinct impression that our hosts were gritting their teeth and using all their willpower not to slap us. We thought it best to go for a walk as we gathered, correctly, that we were far too early and planned to return when peace was restored.

Despite our shortcomings as guests we had a very enjoyable Christmas Eve, with a superb French gastro-feast produced by the lovely Sarina and her husband James. David, James' stepfather, being somewhere to the right of Genghis Khan, was firmly but affectionately put in his place by the other guests before too much damage was done, and before he started banging on about socially taboo areas of our existence. All in all, it was a very happy evening and we all went to bed in a haze of alcohol and goodwill. Even the dog had been forgiven for leaving a small offering of her own in the dining room which some hapless idiot stepped in. It wasn't our fault that he had no shoes on.

Next morning, we were up with the lark to open our pressies with the help of the five-year old Daniel, who proceeded to fling

70

everything around with the sheer joy of being alive at Christmas. My daughter had given us a mysteriously shaped parcel which we were to deliver to James and Sarina. James took the parcel and shook it as one does when testing something. It didn't rattle, so he cautiously unwrapped it to find a three-foot high gleaming fluorescent gnome. James's face was a study. He and his little family live in a tasteful cream and beige London house. He was not going to tolerate a fluorescent green gnome either in the house or in the pretty walled garden.

"Is this some sort of joke," he hissed.

We looked at him and could only agree that it was devoid of any appeal at all. Sarina looked uncomfortable but was unwilling to pass judgement. What could they do? Supposing it was meant to be a serious Christmas present and they had just had lousy taste? How to say thank you for something so gross without throwing up?

"Into the bin with it," announced James. "It's dreadful and I'm not amused. Total waste of money, so in the bin with it."

Then I had my brainwave.

"No," I announced. "It should have a home. It should not be shoved in the bin. It's in such bad taste that it deserves better than that. Ergo, we must find it a home."

We went to the pub to ponder the problem.

The next day, being Boxing Day, we went en famille, to the park at Crystal Palace and spent a tedious hour or three watching small children screaming and running around with snotty noses and generally not being very interesting. The green gnome was in the car awaiting his fate. Having finished watching Danny's prowess on the swings, we decided to head for home and a large, restorative drink.

"James," I said. "I am in charge and I shall look for an appropriate doorway within which to leave the green gnome. It must be the smartest doorway that we can find."

James shook his head.

"Nothing to do with me," he pronounced, "this is all your responsibility. At your age you should know better, but I shall enjoy watching you make an idiot of yourself.

There are a lot of smart doorways in the area around Crystal Palace, so we cruised slowly around in the dusk trying not to look suspicious, until there it was: the perfect doorway. Six large cream stone steps led to a highly glossed black door which was flanked by four beautiful stone pillars.

"Yes!" I cried. "This is it."

Pulling my woolly hat down over my face and wrapping my scarf over my mouth, I climbed out of the car clutching the green monstrosity. Looking around to make sure nobody was watching, I crept up to the gate and lifted the latch. I crept up the path and up the flight of steps. A sudden noise from the bushes around the door made me freeze, but it was only a scrawny old fox hoping for a quick snack. By now all I wanted to do was beat a hasty retreat and, dropping a quick kiss on the green gnome's head, I placed him carefully on the top step and bade him farewell, before turning and charging off down the path to the safety of the car.

Apart from a two-week holiday one summer the Green Gnome remained in situ for nearly three years. I sent him a regular postcard with an update of my life, anonymously of course, so that his new family knew he was not just dumped and he had a story of his own. Maybe the occupants of the very smart house had a sense of humour, or perhaps they thought they'd be jinxed if they dumped him. Who knows?

However, it had to happen and the house went on the market about six months ago and was quickly sold. The next time I passed I stopped and had a chat with the man clearing the garden.

"Did you notice a green gnome in the porch?" I asked.

"Oh yes," he replied. "They've gone to live in France, and they took a really awful green gnome with them. I can't understand why. It was pretty gruesome, but the kids insisted it was packed."

He probably thought I was quite mad when a beam split my face in two. What a very satisfactory ending to know that the Green Gnome of Crystal Palace continues to thrive. I do miss him, though.

YES, I HAVE A FRIEND

Yes, I have a friend.

We sat opposite each other in the small interview room in Swindon police HQ, the girl and I. Her skin was acne scarred, her nose was running and she kept wiping the drips and the tears away with the back of a grubby hand. She was nineteen years old and had been raped. Yes, she was possibly a prostitute but I suppose they are allowed to say no to a client even though the contributory negligence would make one perhaps rather less sympathetic than one might have been had it been some nice middle class girl held at knife point.

But it was not my job to judge. It was my job to create a likeness of the perpetrator with my skill and my tools of the trade, which were just a piece of paper and some pencils. No e-fits then with the potato head and glassy eyes, just honest drawing and an empathy with the victim to be both of comfort and produce the likeness needed. Sometimes it worked better than others. Sometimes the victim cried when the face was seen on the paper which brought back unwelcome memories. Unlike an impersonal computer image, the little old ladies, or the vulnerable wounded girls, or even the men would want to talk, would want to contribute to my drawing, so they had some form of control over what had happened to them.

Slowly, she opened up to me, this grubby, skinny pockmarked girl who was somebody's daughter. She told me of her descent into the murky world of sex with strange men in the back of cars, of the welcome relief of the heroin which blotted out another weary day bringing her nearer to death.

And then came one of the saddest statements I have ever heard, and I've heard many in the course of my work. I asked her if she had any friends who would look out for her, who would try and protect her. Her face lit up.

"Oh yes," she said, smiling, "I have a friend. I don't know his name but he has a red car."

THE FLAVOUR OF THE MONTH

The children ran wild every August. The little ones were egged on by the bigger ones with promises of ice cream if they would all sit in a row in front of Eugene, the band leader who played at the entrance of the big sea water swimming pool, and suck lemons. This sport had the great satisfaction of rendering the brass band incapable of blowing their instruments because of the sudden rush of saliva into their mouths. Eugene would yell at them and chase them away, but in vain. They were always back the next day armed with a fresh supply of lemons. There they would perch, a mass of skinny limbs and tangled salt-filled hair. One day they would be beautiful but for now beauty was the last thing on their minds.

Every morning the occupants of Bungalow number 9 set off from their home wheeling their canoe on its trailer and calling into their mother's grocer where she had an account to stock up with Instant Whip, baked beans and other delicacies to see them through the day. They were lucky at No.9 to have parents who were totally disinterested in what they got up to, so long as they did not drown and reappeared at supper time. The canoe was named Yannick, after a French au pair who would sashay along the sea front, much to the delight of the adults and the boys. She would never go in the water, unlike the feral gang who were in and out of the sea all day long being shouted at by the life guards. The little ones staggered out of the water with the sand filled gussets of their knitted swimsuits hanging down to their knees before emptying out collection of seaweed, water and the odd crab and dashing back in again.

For the slightly older children there was Big Ron for sport. Big Ron was as thick as two short planks but possessed of an admirable physique, which the adoring girls used to like rubbing with coconut oil. He held court on the edge of the pool and occasionally beckon to one of the girls and off they would go in his open top sports car. They would come back bubbling with excitement having been thoroughly kissed. Never anything more. Once they hit sixteen he lost interest.

There was in fact a Mrs. Ron lurking in the background. She ran the naughty postcard shop and had the measure of Ron and kept him out of serious trouble. Then there was cousin Owen who was a vision in white shorts and pristine white shirts, deeply tanned and a dead ringer, so he thought, for Douglas Fairbanks. He was someone's uncle and his arrival from his home in Barbados gave huge kudos to bungalow number 9.

The summer passed. Eugene would gently explain to any little girl who followed him back to his dressing room that it was inappropriate for her to be there. Owen was far too vain to see anything beyond his handlebar moustache and Ron was simply too brain dead to be dangerous, so there was safety there on the South Side. The older girls graduated to home-made bikinis which were cobbled together by some enterprising creature and had a drawstring at each side so they could be raised when there were no adults around, thus giving a much more extensive view of slender thighs. The first proper kiss was given to the tune of Peggy Sue. There was sorrow too, when the object of desire was snaffled by an older child who was the only one of the children to wear a bra. There was no competing with that. Chewing gum was stuck behind the big brother's knees so he could not chase his little sister and the smaller children never wanted to see another lemon.

All things come to an end. Boarding school beckoned and the children scattered to their assorted places of learning. The final Knickerbocker Glory was eaten, the bungalows were scrubbed and emptied of sand and packets of Instant Whip.

The summer was definitely over.

TAXI

I sat in the back of the taxi as it struggled somewhat belatedly through the painfully slow traffic towards Paddington. The gateway to the outside world, Paddington is, the gateway back home to Cornwall, and to other things, to friends and the sea and, of course, the cat Elise. The driver, a large gentleman of foreign lineage with a cheery face, chatted away as I checked yet again in my bag for the tickets, keys, the pills and other detritus of modern life. All was present and correct. Siting back in my seat, I prepared to listen to tales of his wife, his dog, his wayward son, nodding in sympathy as each sorry escapade was aired.

His hand moved towards the radio and there was the voice of Jane Garvey, reporting from Sheffield on matters medical. The topic this particular day was the menopause. To my amusement I noticed the look of bewilderment on the driver's face. There followed several interviews with women who wore their suffering like a badge of honour. With cries of 'oh, the pain! I thought I was going mad' coming from one after another, as well as 'my husband almost divorced me." On and on they paraded the loss of their femininity, the hot flushes, the unexpected flooding at the hunt ball, no less! I began to feel rather irritated. It was not exactly terminal after all. I caught the eye of the driver and grimaced at his reflection.

"Wot dis ting, dis menopause? Queried Billy. It was difficult to see whether he was blushing or not, so I gave him a potted account of what was involved.

"Bet you're learning some new stuff today," I remarked.

Billy was silent for a moment. Then came, "don't dey want man no more?" in a sorrowful tone of voice.

"Oh yes, of course they do," I reassured him hastily. "They just get a bit shriveled up inside.

Silence as the delights of HRT were discussed on the radio. The joys of no more hot flushes, the downsides of depression and suicidal thoughts. It had to be dramatic or there would be no point in the radio programme. Billy began to look rather worried.

"Wot dis HRT ting? Is mah wife gonna kill herself?"

"No, of course not," I told him, hoping I was right.

"wot ah do den, she all dried up, she no want man. Wot ah do, ah need woman fo me," came back Billy's plaintive voice. "She get heddake?"

I decided to take the bull by the horns and put this to bed. I launched into a blow by blow account of the lubricants involved, not being totally convinced he was au fait with it all and ending my instructions with where to get the stuff and where to apply it, just as we arrived at Paddington. Billy turned to take his fare from my hand.

"Tank you fo da information," he said, his teeth very white as he grinned at me. "Yo fit lady, too fit to be all shrivel up. Yo no have menopause fo many years, me tink."

Gee, thanks Billy. Made my day.

IN WHICH FATHER BURKE
RIDES TO THE RESCUE

Once upon a time there was a lonely middle aged priest. He resided at a Doothaboys Hall kind of place up in the hills near Hull, where he apparently guided the lost boys in the right direction, quaffed a great deal of vintage wine and ate wonderful meals which he cooked after a swim in the school pool. Not a bad old life for a man on his own, especially as the priesthood owned a chateau in the Bordeaux region where the religiously inclined could go and pray and do whatever else they did to alleviate any boredom which might set in.

It so happened that Father Burke was a great friend of our heroine's father and would regularly invite her and her then husband to enjoy what he called 'whisky nude evenings.' This involved an evening swim, followed by a very large whisky whilst standing starkers by the fire and then eating the most wonderful food, prepared by himself. Great conversation, wine like nectar; the young couple had indeed arrived. If there was a certain amount of plump hands fluttering around the nether regions of the girl whilst swimming it was most probably accidental as, after all, he was a priest. Having given the youngsters such wonderful evenings it would have been churlish to complain.

This comfortable arrangement lasted a year or so and then the young doctor and his wife left the area and went to live in North Devon. They were very happy there until the young doctor fell ill. In fact, he was very ill and very angry because he suspected he was going to die. For the first time in her life it dawned on his young wife that there was a situation which she could not charm her way out of. She realised she needed help and contacted Father Burke, who was still living the life of Riley in his home for bad boys.

"I will come and comfort you," said Father Burke. "I will come in my trusty blue car and I will wear mufti and your husband won't think I've come because he's going to die. We don't want to upset him, do we?"

'Wonderful,' thought the girl. I need comfort and he is a priest. The husband was still in hospital and was particularly cross that day because there had been a fire scare at the hospital and none of the patients in his ward had been rescued, which he thought was an absolute disgrace, so he was not best pleased when Father Burke turned up. After complaining bitterly about his treatment he allowed Father Burke to say a couple of Hail Mary's over him, although he later told me that it was the quickest blessing on record. We didn't know then that Father Burke had other things on his mind.

The priest came back to sleep at the doctor's house where the wife was making the best of things along with her two children, a boy and girl aged nine and eleven. She showed him to the spare room where he settled in with his luggage. A while later he joined the family for supper. The children were entranced by his stories of the bad boys and the trouble they got into and, as he opened each bottle of wine, he showed them how to present the cork so that people would know the wine was very smart. A happy evening ensued and, eventually, they all went to bed feeling much comforted. Father Burke was a Good Thing.

The next day passed uneventfully. The wife went to the hospital to see her husband, who was still in a bad mood as he was missing the fun. The children went to school, and Father Burke spent the day pottering around and preparing supper, whilst consuming an ever increasing amount of alcohol. It happened to be Barnstaple Fair, an annual event of great local importance. The family babysitter agreed to take Father Burke as well to help her look after the children. Off they went in high spirits, leaving the young wife to think how nice it was to have the company and the fun and how it made things seem a lot better.

Some hours later the babysitter returned with her charges. Far from being aided by Father Burke, he had by this time, consumed so much alcohol that he became stuck in a dodgem car and the whole operation had to be halted whilst he was unwedged and hauled out of danger. The same thing happened on the Noah's Ark roundabout and the babysitter decided to call it a day. She somehow managed to get a sodden Father Burke into her little car along with the children who were ecstatic at how things were panning out. So much fun to see grown-ups behaving so badly. They sang to each other feeling very smug and cheerful.

Supper was somehow produced and eaten. The tired children were allowed to skip a bath and were tucked up by a somewhat subdued Father Burke, who did at least have the grace to feel a little embarrassed about the lapse of behaviour.

The young wife felt oddly peaceful that evening and went and sat by the fire to dream She was going to be able to manage, she felt. She could guard her children and create a new life because she was young and strong. Dreaming away, she did not hear naughty Father Burke come into the sitting room until he stood beside the couch. She was surprised to see that he was wearing a very short blue silk dressing gown which showed his little fat legs and his round stomach. He lowered himself beside her and took her hand. Startled, she turned to look at him just as he clamped her hand firmly down on his genitals and announced that he had come to comfort her.

"Which is your room?" he asked, "I don't want to frighten the children."

"Oh," said the wife. "I don't think so. I have a dying husband and this is in very bad taste. I think it's everybody in their own beds tonight, there's a good chap."

In the morning he came into the kitchen and was unrepentant. He said that priests all had friends whom they comforted. I suspect friends of either sex would be equally useful at giving comfort. He suggested they all go to the chateau to comfort each other. She declined his offer and he left, but not before a half-hearted testing the water type move to grab a breast.

The children were sad not to say goodbye to him. But they helped to clear up a grand total of twenty-three empty wine bottles which they found under the bed, in the bathroom, anywhere and everywhere. The galling part was that her own wine cupboard was also completely empty. He had drunk her out of house and home. But it had had its fun moments, and on a scale of one to ten, it was not so important when a young husband is losing his battle to live and there are little children to look after.

A couple of years' later she was living with a wonderful man and she wrote to Father Burke to tell him she was happy again. A stern letter came back informing her that she was living in sin. She thought this a bit rich and replied to tell him so. She never heard from him again.

SUSAN PENHALIGON REALISES

Susan Penhaligon did not consider herself to be a demanding woman but she was beginning to be disturbed by Mr. Penhaligon's lack of performance in the marital bed. Snoring all the way through Mastermind and then staggering upstairs clutching the night time mugs of hot chocolate was not her idea of a good night. She was tiring of his habit of shouting "I was watching that!" when she made any attempt to turn the television off in order to attract his attention. What to do? One could hardly ask the neighbours.

Susan Penhaligon had had in her lifetime four lovers. She had been married to two of them, and the other two had been married to other people. She was a generous woman who, although not promiscuous, had learned a thing or two along the way about giving pleasure. She was in reasonably good shape if a little worn around the edges and many men would have welcomed her attentions. But not Mr. Penhaligon.

One day Susan Penhaligon sat with her morning coffee in her conservatory pondering her fate. She didn't want to destroy Mr. Penahligon's confidence, which was fragile at the best of times, because she loved him, but nothing she had tried was working. He remained in flaccid state apart from the odd occasion at six o'clock in the morning when his penis took matters into its own hands (not literally) and managed a half-hearted erection.

87

And that was simply not convenient. One had, after all, the dog to let out, the morning cup of tea to be made, the laundry to be sorted and so on and so forth.

Dreaming of long ago orgasms, she came to a decision. Not for nothing was she chair of the WI and a stalwart of the local bowling society. She would take positive action and go on Amazon. Amazon had everything. Amazon would help her.

She looked up sex aids and sat back in amazement as page after page of mysterious implements of torture appeared on the screen before her eyes. She settled on what appeared to be a standard conventional instrument in bright pink, with batteries and which was around, it said, ten inches in length. She thought that should be easily accommodated. The business in hand completed, she prepared herself for her bridge lesson and carried on with her life.

The same but different. Had Brian Penhaligon noticed there was a slightly more emphatic swing to those rounded hips as she went about her household chores? A definite frisson of anticipation.

And so it came to pass that a few days later the postman appeared with a parcel. She snatched it from his hands. Wishing him a hasty goodbye and checking that the man of the house was ensconced with the newspapers and SKY sports, she scuffled upstairs to open her package.

Wow! And wow again! It was huge. No middle class woman of a certain age could take that monster on board, not unless one had been a porn star in an earlier life. And it had suction pads with instructions for a 'hands free' experience. Hands free? How could that possibly work? Could one stick it on the wall and then take a running jump at the thing? She had her Pilates class that morning and, knowing that the instructor was a woman of some experience, she plucked up the courage to ask for some advice. Barely bothering to hide her amusement, the instructor, Debbie, recommended that Mrs. Penhaligon stick it to the washing machine door whilst running a spin cycle and then take a running jump. This was far more complex than Susan Penhaligon had envisaged and she couldn't help feeling a little bit thwarted. She wanted at least a pretence of romance, she wanted to be able to pretend that it was Brian who was ravishing her. Or maybe that Spanish waiter in the hotel dining room storming her bedroom to have his wicked way, having been casting meaningful glances throughout the evening whilst attending her every need.

Reluctantly Mrs. Penhaligon accepted that she was not sophisticated enough to deal with these attachments. They were not seductive. They were far too clinical and unromantic. All she really wanted was to be able to cuddle Mr. Penhaligon and to accept what he had to offer because she really did love him. So she forgot for many months about her plan and gave up trying to seduce Brian Penhaligon. She accepted that she would never have another orgasm, which made her very sad.

Summer came and one day they were have a jolly lunch with old friends and, feeling the effect of several glasses of wine, and knowing that Mary was a woman of experience, Susan plucked up the courage to whisper some words into the ear of her friend.

"Oh, that's no problem," replied the good Mary, after making sure the men were not listening. "You need a Rampant Rabbit. That's what we all have in the Book Club. Just get one of those. Anne Summers. That's where you'll find them."

Susan Penhaligon went home with much on her mind. Summoning the courage, she found the website and there she found her friend. Small and less ambitious, she settled for a more modest model of 6 inches. She stuck to pink and thought it looked friendly and unthreatening. She settled down to routine and waited.

It didn't take long to arrive. The doorbell rang and the village postman stood there. He knew everyone and everyone knew him. Thrusting a package at her with a muttered, "I think this is for you," he leapt back into his van and roared away. She looked at the brown Jiffy bag and gasped. It had been split open down one side and there, unadorned and unrepentant in all its pink glory was the Rampant Rabbit. There was more. Some clown had drawn a smiley face on the side of the package and written the word 'enjoy, Mrs. Penhaligon." For many months after that she hid whenever the postman was around. She eventually heard that he had allegedly tried to hang himself and had been withdrawn from the village postal round.

Some days later whilst watching the cricket one afternoon Mr. Penhaligon was conscious of muffled cries coming from upstairs. Squeaks and squeals could be heard. It didn't disturb him enough to make him leave the cricket and investigate, but he did notice that his wife's cheeks were scarlet and her hair stood on end when she appeared. He asked her what had been going on, but she could only manage, "just a little ironing, dear," as she floated on a cushion of happiness into the kitchen to make a nice cup of tea.

Mr. and Mrs. Penhaligon and the Rampant Rabbit lived happily in perfect harmony for many more years. Mr. Penhaligon regained his confidence now that he was no longer under pressure to perform, and eventually they made gentle and affectionate love and the cocoa was quite forgotten.

DANCING

Little Mrs. Massey loved to dance, but when her husband died she had no one to dance with. Her husband had been an enthusiastic if somewhat embarrassing dance partner. He was the one who is always Dad Dancing and waving his hands in the air to 'Hi Ho Silver Lining,' or worse still singing 'Come On Eileen,' because his cricket team once took a blow up doll named Eileen on a cricket tour. But at least he tried and little Mrs. Massey could do her own thing whilst he sang and waved his arms about.

Eventually, when he was middle aged, because no one is old any more, Mr. Massey passed away. At his funeral everybody sang 'Swing Low Sweet Chariot,' and 'Red Red Wine was played courtesy of his favourite group the Merrymen. Had he been in attendance he would have enjoyed his funeral very much indeed.

Mrs. Massey was lonely and so eventually she sold her big empty house and moved to Cornwall, where she lived in an immaculate road where people were very warm and friendly and seemed to care about her and she was halfway happy. But after a little while, Mrs. Massey thought enough time had passed for her to take up dancing again. She asked around and heard of a lonely widower who sang in a choir, which sounded hopeful as logically he must therefore be musical. Mrs. Massey joined the choir and hated it because she didn't like standing up for two hours and she couldn't read music. She just wanted to dance. She twinkled at Kenneth the widower who twinkled back at her, and she thought 'aha, got him.' One afternoon, on the strength of that twinkling, she approached him and introduced herself and asked him if he liked to dance. But Kenneth backed away in embarrassment, which made poor Mrs. Massey feel like a stalker and the embryonic friendship never recovered.

Mrs. Massey then tried the electrician, a man on his own with three ex-wives but he too declined. Then a new neighbour moved in across the road and Mrs. Massey thought that he might like to go dancing, but no, he didn't want to either. Nor did he want to walk or go to the cinema or the pub, so she stopped mentioning things like that to him and all the other men she came across. She didn't, after all, want to get a reputation! There was one more single gentleman in the pipeline but having loitered meaningfully outside his house a few times she called it a day and realised that she would have to go it alone.

Plucking up all her courage she bought a ticket in advance on the web because she thought that would stop her from chickening out, and one evening she drove through the rain and the dark to Falmouth to the dancing. Her new friends thought this was hilarious but, in fact, Mrs. Massey felt quite proud of herself that he had put her money where her mouth was and was prepared to go it alone.

She had a poor sense of direction but managed to find the Princess Pavilion in Falmouth and parked her little red car up the road for an easy getaway should things not go well. Trotting into the vast hall she felt oddly at home and purchased a large plastic cup of fairly disgusting wine and settled down to people watch. Being far and away the oldest person in the room was not a problem. She was here to dance just like everybody else.

Students milled around wearing tiny skirts and black tights, tiny shorts and leggings, little floppy tops and long fair hair, which they constantly swished back and forth to show the boys how insignificant they were. Gradually, the hall filled up, the enormous tattooed bouncer called Jamie stamped each wrist as it went by and quickly the atmosphere began to change to one of excitement and tension. Smoke poured onto the stage and swirled around in constantly changing colours. More and more of the youngsters edged towards the mosh pit at the front and started calling for the group to appear on stage.

And then! Onto the stage in a cloud of smoke and light bounced the reggae group! All Rastafarians, dread locks and rasta hats. And the crowd went wild. A bit of a warm up followed, and then, oh, the dancing! In her corner she went wild too, twirling and jigging away, waving her arms, oblivious to everything but the beat of the music. On and on she danced until she was exhausted and then, the happiest she had been many a long month, she crept away back to her little red car and drove all the way home singing to herself.

When her neighbours heard, they were amused and a little impressed that she had actually done it on her own. Also, they admired her for her spirit. She had woken up her corner of Cornwall and more than that she had endeared herself to those who were just beginning to get to know her.

All through the summer months she went dancing. Now that she was an old hand she was allowed to park her red car by the main entrance and Jamie the bouncer got to recognise her and to greet her and keep an eye out. There was never an iota of trouble there. She saw no drunken behaviour and was met with nothing but kindness from the youngsters. Gradually the students got to know her too, and became fond of her and bought her drinks sometimes in return for her looking after their coats in the corner where they danced. They didn't invite her to dance because being young, it would have seemed a bit like dancing with your granny and their affection for her didn't stretch to that. But they chatted to her, and they recognized her spirit and they loved her clothes and her funny boots and the fact that she knew the difference between ska and reggae and hip hop and calypso and how to inhale a bit of the weed they offered her without falling over.

Towards the end of the summer, when the nights were drawing in, Mrs. Massey was still dancing on her own. She began to feel a little bit tired of some of the nights and didn't stay until the end. On one of the nights she had a touch of indigestion and had to stop and have a rest until it passed.

The students noticed this and looked out for her even more, because by this time she was their mascot, their lucky charm. This particular evening when the dancing was at its height and the rastas were well away on their own particular cloud of smoke and the arms were waving Mrs. Massey stumbled and became frightened at the noise and the dark and everybody roaring out the words and she thought she needed to leave. A young student took her arm and asked if she was alright. She looked at the student but couldn't see her. She couldn't see anything in fact but could feel the heat and the arms waving and the friendliness and she was content to quit while she could. The student guided her through the crowd back to the entrance where Jamie stood. He took her into his muscular arms ready to take her back to her red car. As she stepped forward into his embrace she felt very safe and it was full of light and she looked into what she felt was the future. She saw Mr. Massey doing his dad dancing with his arms waving and his fingers pointed towards the heavens. Mr. Massey saw her then too, and he stretched out his arms for her and smiled.

"Hurry up," he said, "they're playing our tune."

Mrs. Massey never danced alone again.

MY GRANNY'S LOVE LIFE

Mum always did say my Granny was a drama queen, but nothing could have prepared any of us for the highs and lows of her love life. I mean, I am fifteen years old and up for most things, but there is Granny, at the great old age of seventy something going at it like something out of Love Island, which is pretty disgusting especially when my friend Beth caught the pair of them snogging outside Specsavers. I mean, talk about inappropriate! We laughed, Beth and I, to think that at least they couldn't see each other. Talk about Get a Room. It really is horrible to even think about, them having sex. I mean, they surely must have rusted over by now.

And they look all loved up as well. Maybe I am a bit jealous but they've had their time in the sun, and it's our turn now. Or it would be if Graham would take some notice of me. How come a wrinkled old bat like Granny gets what is actually a pretty hot guy, even if he is ancient, to have some fun with? I bet he knows a thing or two. Yeeeuk. I am not even going to think about it.

Actually, when I do think about it, I reckon Mum's a bit jealous as well as there is a lot of shouting going on at the moment and not much sign of any action in the bedroom. Not that I keep tabs, but it's useful to study the shouty levels sometimes if I want to borrow some money or something, or one of Mum's sweaters.

My friend Beth who works in the Ann Summers shop (yes, I know, we don't get freebies so do NOT ask) was in hysterics when in trots Granny and asks for a mature assistant to serve her. I can understand why she wouldn't like Beth as she is really super glam and would frighten most men off, let alone old ladies. So Beth did a bit of ear wigging and heard Granny muttering something about being out of practice so June, the assistant, took her off to the shelves at the back of the store and Beth hid behind a pile of knickers and stuff and heard June say her stock piece, which goes a bit like this:

"Dipping out toes in the water, are we?" she says in her creepy new best friend voice. She says it puts the customers at ease.

Granny went pink and June proceeded to tell her all about the latest lubricants. One day I shall get Beth to nick some samples. What's the point of not knowing anything when some really hot guy could walk in any day? She got as far as some cream that went all hot when put on the guy's tackle. I mean, yeeeeuk, whoever is going to actually TOUCH it? Nobody does anything so sick as that in real life, surely. Beth should know though, she says nobody buys stuff like that. So why is she telling Granny about it?

Anyway, we didn't hear any more about anything until a few days later Beth and me heard Granny crying in her bedroom. She lives in a really cool house a mile from ours; it's like being on another planet. Clean and really peaceful, whereas ours is all shouty and tense. Granny has lovely bits of furniture, where we just have stuff has usually broken or has lost a leg or something. And my bedroom, I mean, I have to wade through my sister's crap to even get near my door. They keep talking about an extension but pigs might fly, the foundations have been filling up with water all summer long and it's October already. So I like going to Granny's house when she asks me to cat sit her really spoiled designer diva cat. I can have my friends in and pretend it's a flat we share or something. We cook stuff and filch a couple of bottles of wine. One big thing about Granny, she is really generous and easy going about stuff and life and so on. If I thought she knew anything I would ask her advice on boys and clothes, but old people have forgotten everything they ever knew. I mean, what could she tell me that I don't already know?

So there's old Granny crying in her bedroom: so what to do? She does sound a bit upset and sort of hiccuppy and then there's a bit of nose blowing and out she comes, so I have to pretend I haven't noticed anything wrong.

Maybe he has dumped her or something. He's pretty hot for an old man and, although Granny was probably a bit pretty when she was young about a thousand years ago, she does need some ironing now.

Anyway, Granny and I stood there staring at each other and then she really burst into tears and started really sobbing and I thought cripes, whatever do I do now? My friend Beth came in and started hugging Granny really hard which seemed to help. I felt a bit jealous at this bonding thing, after she's MY Granny, not Beth's. In fact, Beth has been getting a bit possessive of my Granny recently. She said my family don't make enough time for her and if she was her Granny she'd be really proud of having someone feisty like that. It's better than her Gran who just sits and moans about her ailments all the time. I've told her lots of times that we are busy and if she doesn't ask for anything it means she doesn't need anything and, anyway, she's got the Colonel, which is my name for her chap whose real name is Arthur. I mean, what a name! I'd rather die than go out with someone called Arthur. But I suppose beggars can't be choosers at that age because they are all popping off.

That is what they are meant to be doing, I mean. My dad says they're all living too long and taking up our generation's pensions, which isn't fair all, because they've had it good for years. Just 'cos they fought a bit in the war doesn't excuse the fact that they've lived too long and take up too much space, which we need for our own kids. Not that I'm going to have any. All that screaming and pain, God, no thanks. I'll get a surrogate or best friend to have it for me. I wonder if Beth would do it?

Granny is now sobbing into Beth's new sweater which will really bug her. She's really anal about her clothes, even if she is my best friend.

"Tell me what the problem is," says Beth in a creepy voice like her mother uses sometimes on the younger kids.

"It's Arthur," sobbed Granny. "He says we're too old, and he's too old and people will think we are sad old fools and that everyone will laugh at us, but I really love him. We have so few years left, why can't we just enjoy them in peace? We have such fun. We do a lot of cuddling (hang on Granny, too much information) but he feels that it's too late for us to be together and he's embarrassed because he's has a lot of wrinkles. But so have I, and I love his wrinkles. Now he's left me and I shall never see him again because I won't be able to play croquet now without crying if I see him."

On and on she went, poor old thing. I went to make a cup of tea, which was all I could think of doing. Beth seemed to have it all under control anyway. I felt a bit left out, if truth be told. She was talking to Beth so easily and Beth seemed like the grown up.

Suddenly she came through to the kitchen and whispered, "quick, get out into the drive. Arthur is sitting in his car. For heaven's sake go and get him to come back. Stop looking like a prat and DO something!"

I felt like telling her to piss off and stop interfering. Who does she think she is? Granny will be okay in the morning; she just needs a good night's sleep. In fact, I must have said it out loud because Beth looked at me as if she really didn't like me. A look which made me feel a bit ashamed.

Off I went to find Arthur, who was huddled in his car. Sitting there, sobbing into a clean white hanky. Of course, it would be clean, him being in the army and all that. I get so sick of his army stories. I mean, just because they won a few battles and got killed a bit. Stuff happens. Now MY generation have really got it bad, what with no jobs and having to pay for college and all that crap. Some politicians have got the right idea. Free uni's, free NHS and free travel if we want to go and live in, say, France. Not that I would, but we should be allowed to if we want. It would mean learning the language, which would be a step too far, really. They should just take us and be glad to have us.

Anyway, by this time I had reached Arthur, who carried on sobbing. It was really sad, because I have never seen a grown man up close crying before. I patted his arm and he straight away turned his face into my shoulder. It felt really nice and natural so I patted him again and asked him what I could do to help.

"I love her," he sobbed, getting louder and louder. Luckily there was nobody around to hear the rumpus. I mean, it was a bit embarrassing, him being so old and all that stuff. "I love her, but I've sent her away because I thought we were too old for Ann Summers and making love and being together for what time we have left."

The sobs became even louder. Suddenly, I kind of knew what to do. Beth was right.

"GO AND TELL HER!" I yelled at him, making him jump.

"But I sent her away," he muttered.

"She's crying in the kitchen," I said and then shouted, "GO!!"

Hi face lit up.

"Is she really?" he asked, as if afraid of the answer.

"She loves you," I told him and then he was gone.

I didn't realise an old geezer could move so quickly as I watched him rocket up the garden path and into Granny's house. I saw her turn and take him in her arms with a smile which lit up the whole world, a smile which was also on his face. A lovely, kind, tanned face which had its own history. A face which had seen bravery and loss without complaint. A face which belonged to a man who loved my Granny and made her happy.

I felt a little ashamed at the cavalier attitude with which my generation had written off so much without a glimmer of understanding and I was proud to be a witness at their wedding two months later. Watching the bridal car being driven away I felt honoured to have witnessed not only their wedding, but their love for one another. And I hope Ann Summers's profits went sky high.

SURGEON'S CONSULTING ROOM

Scene: Surgeons' consulting room in a private hospital in Bath.

Dr. Paul Maddox eyes the frightened woman sitting opposite him. She is beginning to cotton on to the fact that all is not well.

"Is your husband in the building?" he asks her. "If so, I think he should be here."

"He's in reception," answers the woman.

Dr. Maddox buzzes the receptionist and very soon the husband enters the room looking terrified. He sits down and takes his wife's hand.

"I'm afraid the news is not good," begins Dr. Maddox. "You have a grade three tumour in your right breast, which I'm afraid means radical surgery as soon as possible."

The husband goes green and passes out on the floor.

"But I have ten people coming to dinner tonight," says the woman.

"Well, I suggest you cancel them," replied the doctor.

"Oh no," says the woman, "I never, never cancel a party. It must go on."

"I really do think you should cancel it," the doctor insists, even though he realises that she won't listen to him.

The doctor outlines the plans for surgery in a week's time. The woman watches dispassionately whilst first aid is given to her husband. When he is upright and reasonably sensible they drive slowly home, having set the date for the operation.

Deep in thought; deep in shock. That was the bad news.

Three weeks later Dr. Maddox asked the woman whether the party went well.

"Oh yes," she said. "It was a very special night. Lots of laughter and lots of tears."

Two weeks later she is sitting opposite the oncologist, a somewhat joyless chap, but I don't suppose his job is a bundle of laughs. They are discussing chemo. To have or not to have. The woman studies the oncologist and weighs up in her mind what her choices are. But there is another choice which has not been mentioned. A risk, but nevertheless, a choice.

She breathes deeply and says, "If I said to you I would rather be in a wine bar drinking wine than having chemo, would you say I was a stupid woman?"

"No," he replied, not looking at her. "I would not."

He looked up but she was gone. Quick as a flash out of the door.

"Send me the bill," she called out as she disappeared down the corridor.

Fifteen years later she is still around annoying everybody and there is a bit more good news. Our heroine can now paint behind the boiler, and the old guy who groped her on New Year's Eve had a lovely time which cost her nothing.

SUNDAY(S)

Why is it so often Sunday? Saturdays are just the lead in time to Sundays, but at least on Saturdays one can go out for a nice lunch or retail therapy and it's not taboo to telephone someone for a dog walk or something.

There must be thousands of lonesters who struggle through Sundays, willing the day to hurry up and go quickly and which are made worse at this time of year as there is absolutely sod all on the telly. I remember just after my husband died, and when I was still living in Wiltshire before decamping to Cornwall, thinking 'oh, I have almost done with these awful Sundays because I am moving to Cornwall and my daughter will take care of me on Sundays with Happy Family Days Out, frolicking on the beach with picnics and happy dogs, just like in the magazines. Dream on. Everyone works full time, so Sundays are catching up days, sleeping days, sorting out problems with offspring days, running said offspring hither and thither days with a scratch supper, at the end of a busy Sunday, whilst proud granny (and many other proud elderly people) are eating their soft boiled eggs of a Sunday evening and thinking 'if I go to bed at half past eight, that's another Sunday over with.'

I mentioned this to my son at Christmas once when nostalgia overtook me and I freely admit I did do the Sad Widow bit once too often. His reaction was one of exasperation at my moaning and he told me in no uncertain terms that I could not expect to be invited to Sunday lunch every Sunday as I had to understand that they are all VERY BUSY!

So, I sat down and thought on one of those long Sundays and came up with the answer. In order to survive and in order to find a voice, I had to make my own way with friends of my own age.

I did exactly that, and I survived. And there was a moment of sheer glee when I realised that last New Year I had three party invitations and my son and daughter only had one.

That said, I still have trouble with Sundays. The cinema, drink, sobbing. I have tried them all. What we Saddoes need is a partner in crime, another single mate, preferably of the opposite sex, to have fun with. And a boat. There is little point in moving to Cornwall and not having access to a boat. Any offers?

RANDOM ACTS OF KINDNESS

I have Parkinson's. There, I have said it.
I am used to saying it now. I accept this is who
I am. I am a freezer, not a shaker (far more
interesting) and because I do not shake and
look incredibly healthy it takes people by
surprise. They do not see the constant battle
between myself and the Frozen Goat, so named
after a herd -flock?- of goats who, when
alarmed, roll over and stick their legs in the
air.

Each morning I awake and wonder what
the Goat is going to do, how far I am going to
be able to walk today, which tricks I can fool it
with. I have tried cajoling, threatening,
coaxing, walking backwards (that worked for a
while) hopping, you name it and as fast as
something works the Goat will eventually see
through it and go on strike.

So that is my life. It is a good life with
plenty of laughter but I have to say the Goat
ain't getting any better. Various doctors have
despatched me to various departments as they
try to work out my modus operandi. I tell them
that I must be the only patient they have who
would love something terminal where I could
lie around for six months dispensing largesse
with everyone running around having to be
nice to me. I announced that I had no
intention of crawling around with damp
knickers, which galvanised them into sending
me to a couple of counsellors, both of whom
pronounced me far too well balanced to need

their services. So here I am. I no longer cry. I accept my fate and am relentlessly cheerful. Even my doctor says he cannot decide whether it's an act or a genuine state of mind. I can't answer that because I don't know myself.

A couple of weeks ago I decided a trip into Truro would be a good idea. Truro is lovely and I enjoy going there. Arriving at the car park all was well. I parked in the blue badge space and set off in the direction of the ticket machine. Now, when approaching said machine the legs will regularly go on strike. They have their favourite places to go on strike. The trick is to stand gazing into the distance as though waiting for someone and allowing everyone to take my place in the queue whilst muttering something about not being in a hurry so, please, do go ahead. One can only keep saying this for a maximum of half an hour before people begin to wonder what I'm about to do. The first act of random kindness came about when an extremely attractive gentleman came to my rescue, paid for my ticket, took it to my car, returned with my keys and announced that he would be back in one hour and if I was still there he would put me back into my car.

Staggering around the corner, I made it to the entrance of M&S and promptly came upon hurdle number two. My path was littered with hazards that day. Stripes. People like me can't do stripes. Or swirly carpets. Or doorways. Or a load of other things come to that. I stalled in the entrance, managing to cause a pile up behind me. What to do? I was well and truly stuck this time, until a large ginger haired woman seized my arm and announced that she was from the social and knew all about people like me and where did want to go? I settled for the Food Hall, so off we went. She cleared the path ahead like whatshisname and the parting of the Red Sea. She attached me to a trolley and bade me farewell after more offers of assistance. I shall never mock fat ginger haired people ever again.

Then the fun really kicked in. The trolley went one way and the Goat said 'no' and went in the opposite direction. So there I was, stretched out like those cartoons when some idiot is about to fall into the river, when a nice M&S lady started to laugh and said, "Are you alright dear?"

"Not really," I replied and started to laugh because the only alternative was to cry and I've done enough of that.

And so began the next of several acts of random kindness from strangers who for half an hour became my closest friends. The nice lady plonked me in a chair, took my shopping list and returned with everything I asked for. I gave her my wallet because I trusted her absolutely and she paid for it. Enter the red-haired woman again, who seemed to want to take possession of me, but I managed to convince her I was really okay. Not.

We then had to pause and work out how to get me to my car. Two youthful employees dressed in black were summoned to assist and they kind of half carried me plus trolley all the way back to the car park. They loaded everything including me into the correct places. They wouldn't even take any money for their troubles and simply smiled and went on their way. Their mothers would be proud of them.

I bet everyone thought I was being arrested for shoplifting, but I didn't actually care. And as soon as I got home my legs said to themselves 'hey ho, that was fun, let's behave ourselves for a while now," and they walked, good as gold, into the sanctuary of my little sun filled house.

Bastards.

(By the way, if you are wondering, my driving is not affected...yet).

THE MAN WHO WORE RED SHOES

The woman followed the porter to her room. It was a pretty room in a very upmarket hotel renowned for its gardens and its restaurant, which is just what the woman, whom we shall call Sarah, wanted. In fact, needed. She had been ill for what seemed a very long time and was here to sleep and eat delicious food and be looked after.

Having showered and changed into something more elegant, for she was an elegant woman despite the ravages of the disease she was struggling with, and she was a proud woman, she picked up her bag and keys and went downstairs to the bar. The underemployed barman was trying hard to look busy, and a fire hissed and spat in the grate as the raindrops fell down the chimney. It was a large room and very empty, as it would appear that only five people were staying. Large comfortable sofas were grouped around with smaller armchairs, and the bright fire threw out a considerable heat despite the rain hissing on the logs.

Sarah took her place in an armchair by the fire and ordered a Campari soda. The barman chatted away, having only been in the job for a week after four years living in China until his romance went wrong. What stories people have to tell! There is always an element of surprise which catches the listener unaware, always something brave or stupid or exciting that the storyteller had done to escape or to survive.

An elderly gentleman hobbled slowly into the bar on a stick with a silver head. Of course, it would have a silver head as its owner was a man of some style, although in his eighties. He lowered himself onto a sofa on the other side of the fire to the woman and proceeded to complain about his lunch, the hotel staff, the weather, in fact anything he could think of. He had a bottle of red wine already opened and was busy working his way through it. Sarah rather wished she had done the same but it was too late as her white wine had been poured and was en-route to the dining room.

She nodded at the elderly gentleman, and began to speak until he cut her short.

"No, don't speak to me. I don't want to talk to anyone," he grumped. "Without wishing to be rude, I am not in the mood for conversation."

Fair enough thought the woman called Sarah. Win some, lose some. She caught sight of his red socks with perfectly matched red smoking slippers and decided that although he looked interesting it wasn't really worth the effort of the chase. She finished her Campari and set off for the dining room.

Four other people were in the restaurant, both couples. Then the old man came in and proceeded to give the waitress enough grief to make a lesser girl want to hit him. He complained about the lighting, the

113

service, his choice of food. The waitress obviously had his measure and fielded his moaning with good humour and charm. Sarah finished her meal and, feeling less than her usual sociable self, took her book and reclaimed her seat by the fire along with an Amaretti on the rocks. Curled up as she was, she did not realise that old red socks had returned and taken up his spot on the other side of the fire. Silence reigned. Ten minutes passed. He cleared his throat and announced to the empty bar, "I am not intending to be rude, but I really do not want to talk to anyone."

This was obviously his mantra for the evening. Sarah nodded and replied that she felt the same and just wanted to read her book. End of conversation.

A log bounced into the hearth and both of them jumped.

"Bloody logs," announced old red socks.

Sarah ignored him.

Where do you live?" came suddenly from across the hearth.

Sarah looked up in surprise. "Just a few miles away. I'm here for a rest."

"I can't hear you," he said. "Come and sit by me."

She crossed the carpet and perched beside him. The barman watched them with his mouth hanging open. Mr. red socks began to talk and told her why he was there. Marooned in the hotel whilst his wife was in a nearby nursing home probably dying,

114

Marooned because his home was in Antibes and she was taken ill in Cornwall. Miserable, lonely, bored and worried. He told her about his life, his businesses, the people he hated (nearly everyone) his family. He talked for over two hours and for two hours Sarah listened. The barman was astounded. The bar was deserted and more Amaretti was drunk as the conversation became more personal and the pair of them became more tactile. Nothing sleazy, just affection and the pleasure of each other's company.

Eventually Sarah stretched. She had been ill for a long time and it was taking its toll. She leaned over to kiss him goodnight and the naughty man proffered his lips instead of a cheek. In fact, he proffered his lips quite a few more times and because she liked him very much she kissed him back.

"You have made my day," he said.

They never did learn one another's names. It didn't seem important. As far as I know they ever met again because early next morning Sarah departed the hotel in an ambulance, having been taken ill in the night. I do know that as she lay in bed, in a great deal of pain, she thought that if it was to be her last night on earth the it could not have been a happier one.

MODERN MANNERS

Once upon a time an elderly lady availed herself of a creole fish cake. She sat on a low stone wall in the sunshine near Sloane Square, where generally one meets a better class of person. She was contentedly filling in time before adjourning to the Royal Court Theatre for one of their thought provoking plays which they do so well.

Sitting in the sunshine, she bit into the fish cake and very good it was too. She would normally have gone to one of the smart restaurants around Sloane Square but the Parkinson's was a bit temperamental that day, and restaurants are crowded, so there she was, sitting on the wall. She felt a rustling near her left shoulder and turned to see a small boy with the usual green snotty tramlines running down his chin. He watched her carefully and made a small noise indicating that a bite of the fish cake would go down well with him. The elderly lady shook her head, and said quite pleasantly "run away, there's a good chap," which had no effect on him whatsoever. Slightly more firmly she said, "go away, there's a good boy, I'm trying to enjoy my fish." Like a small puppy, he obeyed and trotted along the top of the low wall to where his parents and little sister were busy unpacking their own picnic lunch.

She heard the Mummy asking the little boy, "what did the lady say to you, darling?"

"She told me to go away, Mummy," said the little boy and our elderly lady's heart sank.

Sure enough, up zooms Mummy in her camel hair coat and expensive shoes, and the conversation went thus:

Mummy: "You told my son to go away. You must be sick. Have you got grandchildren?"

Elderly Lady: "Yes, I have."

Mummy: "and would you tell them to go away?"

E.L.: "Yes, I would if they were annoying me."

Mummy: You must be sick. You're a miserable old woman and I hope you die!"

E.L.: That's a bit strong, isn't it?

Mummy: I hope you die, and before you die, I hope you have even more miserable years!"

Clutching the little boy by the hand, she races off to Sloane Square to spend some money.

E.L.: "That was a bit strong, wasn't it? These mothers..."

Before she could finish, the husband turned to her and shouted, "That is my wife you're talking about. You have offended our son. He's only four and you've offended him."

E.L.: "Well, your son has offended me by snotting into my fishcake."

Husband: "Get a life!" he said, before storming off after his wife.

At least the old woman had the satisfaction of spoiling their lunch, but, actually, they had spoiled hers too. If we can never chastise our children in case they are offended, what hope is there that they will grow into balanced adults? The unnerving thing is that, although entertaining enough, the protagonists were so middle class, even upper middle, I would say. People aren't meant to behave like that. The British are usually more polite than most, and would not normally stick their heads above the parapet. But maybe nowadays everyone is aware of their rights and not their responsibilities. I think the parents should have told the child that the nice lady was eating her lunch, so leave her alone.

Having said that, the same elderly lady, when shopping in Peter Jones' and when two small children were driving her nuts by running round and round one of those whirligig display things, somehow managed to inadvertently to stick out her foot so that the smaller child, whizzing around the corner, tripped and sailed through the air, landing with a thud several feet away. She beat a hasty retreat with a smile and a shrug of her shoulders.

I HEARD IT ON THE NEWS

A friend of mine heard it on the news and rang to tell me that she had an interesting job for me. The gentleman concerned had survived his third trial for allegedly bashing his foster daughter with a tent peg, thereby bringing her life to a premature end. His first conviction was deemed unsafe and so the old legal system ground into action and, with two subsequent trials, both of which resulted in a hung jury. After eleven years our gentleman was finally free to walk the streets again and free to marry his devoted lady admirer who was, as luck would have it, extremely wealthy as well as besotted.

Having had eleven years to ponder his future, Shaun as I shall call him, decided that suddenly he had total recall and that there had been a shifty looking individual in the house who was obviously the killer. Shaun was demanding that a police artist be used in conjunction with his appearance on TV to promote "The Book Which Would Prove His Innocence."

That is where I came in. It was arranged for me to meet Shaun and Mrs. Shaun in the Hotel Du Vin in Winchester. We were then to move to another hotel where the crew were waiting to film the whole thing. I would be filmed drawing from Shaun's description and he would be filmed looking angst ridden and badly done by. The whole lot would go on air as a sort of 'saving Shaun' exercise.

I waited in the lounge of the hotel. And waited. Just when I was beginning to feel annoyed in bound a tall, attractive man wearing the standard Wiltshire mufti of striped shirt, navy blazer and chinos. He was followed by a very pretty woman in a long floaty dress and rather nice boots. We decided to have coffee. Conversation flowed easily and I found myself enjoying his company. He was educated and charming, as was his wife, Fiona. They were very tactile with one another. She obviously adored him and I could feel myself warming to them both.

We drank our coffee and adjourned as planned to another hotel just up the road where the crew were waiting. Sandwiches were laid out and I was given a large table upon which to work. To begin with there was a certain amount of suspiciously rehearsed hesitation to make it appear more authentic, and then Shaun was in full flow.

Pacing the floor, face wracked with pain, our Shaun gave it his all. I think he had convinced himself of his own innocence and on and on he went. Every detail, every detail of facial hair, every inch of the perpetrator's face was recalled. He strode, he strutted, he wrung his hands, he produced tears until I had eventually finished the drawing and showed him. He had obviously done his research as victims often cry when the image is completed, usually in relief that they can move on, that they have somehow handed the memories and the fear over to someone else. So Shaun wept and mopped his handsome face while his wife gazed in adoration.

I didn't believe a single word of it.

I was speaking to his wife later when he came and put his arm around her.

"Darling," he said, "we must go. Our train is due shortly."

He shook my hand and made his farewells to one and all, his voice trembling with emotion.

Nobody spoke. I think we were all dazed at the bravura performance. As I drove out of Winchester I passed them walking to the station. I noticed that he strode ahead, leaving her scurrying behind in her pretty dress and boots. There was a coldness between them which had not been apparent during the interview. A coldness from him to her. She had served his purpose.

The TV channel would appear to have had the same thought as the whole programme was dropped. My interest in the case was the ease with which one can talk, laugh and enjoy the company of a complete rogue. Or perhaps my standards are dropping.

THE MAN WHO COULD NOT BE HUGGED

The widow never meant to have a lodger. She was certainly solvent but liked to pretend otherwise. It was just one of those throwaway remarks which can come back and bite you on the bum. They had been ambling along, two women who had been friends since forever, when the Widow remarked that having a lodger must be a nice little earner, what with having all that lovely cash every month....

"Try it," said sensible Ruth, who had a lovely husband and two lovely well married daughters who came to see their mother every weekend and behaved exactly as they should.

The following week there was a knock at the door. Our heroine had of course forgotten all about her conversation with Ruth and greeted the man with her usual over-the-top enthusiasm. She saw a weary man whose face gave the appearance of having lived more lives than its owner. His grey hair grew in little spikes which had rebelled against any attempts to brush it into some sort of order. He had blue eyes which, later when he was more settled, would sparkle with humour. Behind him in the driveway was a beautiful gleaming white Mercedes. The widow's eyes lit up when she saw it. She smiled to herself as she imagined summer evenings touring the Cornish countryside, scarves trailing Isadora Duncan style, waving gaily at lesser beings as they flew past.

He moved his few belongings into her house and before very long they were off, trading stories of lives well lived, lovers lost, coffee growing cold as they talked. Two pairs of eyes alight with mischief, delighted at having discovered a partner in crime.

The lodger's tales were of drunken antics, of women abandoned, of macho adventures, of a trail of broken hearts left in his wake. The widow's were more circumspect. Her heart had been wounded not so long ago and she needed security more than love.

The lodger sensed this and backed off hastily where once he might have struck. But he was sensitive beneath his bravado and he helped her as much as he could. He did the shopping and took the cat to the vet when she was suffering a bout of chronic constipation. (The cat, not the widow) and made himself useful in all sorts of ways.

It is only fair at this point to say that the Widow was not quite as she seemed. An appalling flirt, she loved parties and hers were legendary. She loved to tease the paper-man by wearing a frilly nightie when he arrived each morning, she kissed the EDF man (he looked lonely), she put up little notices telling the world to knock and come in. All around the house were jokes; Valerie the hen, a reindeer named Jennifer, little jokes with which to tease her guests, a child's pirate rug on the floor, candles drooping in the sunshine looking grotesquely phallic, snippets of letters, photos of husbands one and two. Everything had its place and its story, some true, some less so.

Needless to say, the lodger loved it. Loved the water sparkling in the sunshine, loved her stories. It mattered not one iota if they were true or not, her role was to provide a place where friends could drink wine and relax. He felt immediately at home and their evenings, if there was no football, rugby or cricket to watch, were spent talking and drinking wine, but mostly they laughed and laughed.

And because she was having such fun and because she was delighted with his company so much the Widow made her mistake. She flung her arms around him when he gave her a fistful of banknotes. He was mortified and tried desperately to escape, protesting as he fled that it was a business agreement and was nothing more. For all his laughter and warmth, the lodger did indeed hate to be hugged.

That evening the Widow asked the Lodger (by now fortified by wine) what he wanted from her.

"I need a quiet room in which to watch football and peace and quiet to sort out my life," he replied.

"Oh," said the Widow. "I want the opposite. I want my own playmate. To go to parties with and drive around the Cornish countryside with and to kiss me goodnight."

The Lodger eyed her and said, "well, we were doomed from day one. You are the worst landlady in the whole of Cornwall. You are not allowed to say you hate my boots and furthermore if you were a man you'd be had up for sexual harassment."

There was a twinkle in his eye as he came to the last bit. The Widow allowed her bottom lip to tremble, but he ignored it. Been there before. A tear ran down her face and he softened a tiny bit.

"You need a man," he said, "but it can't be me."

He mentioned one of her admirers but her face fell.

"You must be joking," she fumed. "He doesn't make me laugh and he blows his nose on his napkin."

To avoid further misunderstanding the Lodger made up the following rules:

1/. Thou shalt not embrace the Lodger when being paid lots of cash. It's a business relationship and nothing more.

2/. Thou shalt not waylay the Lodger on his way to bed muttering "give us a kiss, big boy."

3/. Thou shalt not skip around wearing nothing but a towel.

4/. And worst of all, on no account shall you be allowed to hug the Lodger. No cuddling up in the evenings watching Silent Witness or having her feet rubbed. No sharing a goodnight kiss at bed time.

The Widow was frankly appalled. Everyone she knew did hugs. How on earth could one share a life without hugging? She cried, but to no avail. He said "it's not in the contract." She grumbled and met the same response. She tried patting him as she passed, so he banned her from sharing the sofa. Finally, sadly, she capitulated. She became subdued and quiet. The fun was gone. She didn't understand how he could show affection without hugs.

She freely admitted she was a hopeless landlady. She cooked him food until he begged her to stop mothering him. She failed to appreciate that his room was his sanctuary. She told him she hated his boots.

Slowly she came to realise that she had no option but to abide by his rules, and off they went again on the merry go round of banter and laughter; teasing, provoking, trying to forget the very tragedies that had brought them together. Deceased spouses? Four between them! Terrible track record. One or other would quip to lighten the moment, daring any of their friends to feel pity. Pity was to be avoided at all costs.   After   some months of this the Widow began to want her house back. She found living without hugs so alien that she became more and more confused as to how to be with him, when in fact all the poor man wanted was a bed and board and some time to get his life sorted out. He wanted to return to South Africa where the sun shone all day and where he could remember being happy. The Widow's friends were kind enough but they were not his friends, and he kept more and more to his room, longing for the warmth of the sun on his back.

The Widow was the first to give in. She announced somewhat tactlessly that he was to leave at the end of the month. The Lodger, unsurprisingly, was annoyed. He had been flawless in his behaviour and he would not be held hostage because some wretched woman wanted his body, his soul and anything else she could lay her hands on. He stuck to his guns and increased the leaving time to two months in the hope it would convince her that they worked well together, hugs or no hugs.

The strange thing was that he missed her. Missed her laughing at him, missed her curled up on the couch carefully not touching him, missed her rude stories and her ability to laugh at herself. His fortunes had turned around, he found a new life and a new wife but he still missed her. One day, over on business and almost without thinking, he found himself outside her pretty house in Cornwall. Knocking on the door, calling out her name as she was there, her little red car was there. After what seemed forever, her old friend Ruth came out to see who it was.

"Oh, oh," she exclaimed, "how lucky you're here!"

It transpired that the Widow had never put up the railings to stop her from falling over and, true to form, clutching her trademark bottle of wine, she had fallen head over heels into the rockery, just as she said she would do when the fun stopped being fun.

"Watch me fall," she would cry, and managed to never to spill a drop as down she went.

He crept into her pretty bedroom where she lay and was shocked at her frailty. She looked at him standing there so big and strong and she smiled.

"Ah," she said, "have you come to give me a hug?"

"Yes," he replied. And so he did.